Hi

God

How

Are

You

MANOJ KUMAR SHARMA

Dedication

This novel is dedicated to
"Vasudhaiv Kutumbkam."

Special Thanks

To all the book lovers, readers, reviewers, critics, and literature houses who loved my earlier books –

MIRRRO, *Me No Pause Me Play*,

and

JUUHHHUUUU

and inspired for more and more story telling.

Contents

Acknowledgements

Thanks from the bottom of my heart....

- To my nation "India"
- To All Indians
- To All 8 Billion People on Earth

Synopsis

Vasudhaiva Kutumbakam

अयं निजः परो वेति गणना लघुचेतसाम् ।
उदारचरितानां तु वसुधैव कुटुम्बकम् ॥

Ayam Nijah Paro Veti Ganana Laghucetasam
Udaracaritanam Tu Vasudhaiva Kutumbakam

Small-minded discrimination, saying that one is a relative and the other is a stranger.
Magnanimous conscious belief that the entire world is its own family.

The original verse from Chapter 6 of Maha Upanishad VI.71-73, later highlighted in Bhagavad Gita and in today's age, is piously engraved at the entrance hall of the Parliament Of India.

This unchallengeable timeless doctrine evolved from the holiest place on Earth, Jambudvipa/ Aryavarta/ Bharat/ Hindustan/ India, chronologically enlightened many across geographical contours and still in today's age influencing masses as the only route for inclusive global peace and prosperity.

Unfortunately, the ground reality is immensely contradictory.

Every now & then, every here & there Wars are being orchestrated for the dire reasons of miraged horizons aspirations for acquiring domination over parts of the world or the whole world..... Wars of nations, wars of religions/faiths, wars of cast/color/creed, wars of egos and ethos?

Right Time never comes! This is the right time!!

Don't think, debate, and preach only! Let's act cohesively to transfer a livable place on Earth for our coming generations to have peaceful and prosperous co-existence forever……else they will never forgive us……

CHAPTER 1

Hi God! How are you?

First Reel - Fairy Whines

03rd December

Sometimes in future.......

A reel from Indra Prasth Nagar, the capital of Bharat, was posted on social media.

Hi God! How are you?
I am not well, how do you do?
My Mom & Dad always pray you.
But, I don't! I just love you! Do you love me too?
They say, you are Lord of everything,
But, I wanna ask you many things.
Hi God! Why I born abnormal?
Is it okay or another new normal?
When Doctors lost hopes for me,
Then why they say God may help me?
I am alone, no brother or sister.
Can you be my brother or sister?
No children play with me, don't know why?
Please come, play with me, I wanna run & fly.
Answer me, what is in your mind?
Don't stay deaf, dumb and blind.
I am counting now, one...two...three....
Hmmm! Okay!! Call me when you will be free.....

∀ **Hooponopono**

- Oh! Mamma!! What's this? For the first time in my life, I saw somebody calling God like this....Interesting BTW

That was the first-ever reaction to the reel posted a few minutes back on ∀.

∀ It is the latest app in the market, and it has grown exponentially beyond the sky since its launch, beating all historical records and leaving all apps way behind, including e-commerce, social media, government body apps, and many more. It has unique USP(s) attributing to OS, devices, locations, navigations, memories, security, user loyalty etc.

∀ Is designed in such a unique, intelligent way that unlike few others, it can be run on any available or even any future operating platforms – likes of iOS & all Apple platforms, Android, Windows, macOS, Chrome OS, Ubuntu, Red Hat Linux, Oracle Linux, CentOS, Kali, IBM, Fedora, Debian, SUSE, and many more in the dynamically updated long list in the market.

∀ Is designed so smartly using innovative algorithms enabled through AI, Chatbot, Electroencephalography and CII (Cosmos Infinite Intelligence), which can redesign itself randomly while in use, as per user's requirement.

∀ Empowers the user with never seen before facilities as it can be used in any device or machine – mobile phones, notepads, MacBooks, laptops, palmtops, desktops, wristwatches, any type of TV Screens, commercial digital screens, billboards, and even in virtual reality invisible screens. And more over the same user can parallelly operate, ∀ at the same real-time in all the devices and machines she or he owns with fairly matching resolutions.

The next unique capability of ∀ is that it works on both online and offline modes, and, in circumstantially life-threatening scenarios, it influences nearby devices by using GPS to get on to guide for help in saving the lives of the sufferer.

One never before application has, even if the devices are in off mode or sleep mode, and it is always alive like clocks. That enabled the app to sense and scan the behavior of trees, animals, and birds prior to natural calamities like earthquakes, cloud bursts, floods, cyclones, storms, etc.

∀ Don't depend on any external cyber security provider's services. It has its own built-in algorithm for the overall security of the device, app, and user. It not only protects defensively against any external cyber-attack but acts on the principle of 'Attack is the best defense,' offensively travelling to the source device & software and destroying them there only without any scope of survival. Before displaying, it scans the inputs through its own malware, which travels into the source domain and if free from any illegal, harmful intent and genuine as per updated guidelines, then only allows for harmless & user-friendly display.

Wherever it is alive in devices, it initiates talks with all other existing platforms, apps and befriend them to follow ∀ as the Boss.

In a very short period of time, it took over real, cyber, virtual reality, AI, and CI globally, as well as even interstellar destinations.

One more unique feature it offered, the user need not to worry often for drain out of battery and charging for the device. ∀ utilise the body of device and uses heat of solar energy or light energy of various light sources like LED or other lamps, user's own physical & mental energy to charge the same conventional trending batteries in markets.

∀ Don't always ask the user for a password. Soon after a few uses, once habituated, without asking the password, it uses thermal radiations, touch senses, and face & eye scans as automatic login. The user does not need to scan and save those personal vital features, but this app, by default, collects all those data for the first few uses. If tried by another user, it locks the whole system and informs the user through other devices like home TV, PC, Laptop or any other, and unlocks itself until the real owner regains control.

∀ comprehensively keep vigil over everything going around and pick selective content published on any other app or platform based on its holistically designed merit criteria screening. If some users, as regular loyal users of any other app or platform, post the content, they may be randomly picked up by ∀, even if they are not subscribers. On the other hand, if a ∀ user's post deserves as per ∀'s SOP, then it may be posted on other relevant matching apps. Apart from technical competency, ∀ it has collaborated with all available apps in the market to facilitate this wonderful facility. If a user of ∀ doesn't have any other app, then they also can post the content on all other apps in one click with ∀ ID.

∀ Its collaboration with all other apps and its peculiar design enables the user to not worry about installing those apps separately. The user has to search by typing the name of the app in ∀ the portal, and it will automatically connect with that app through the user's ∀ ID.

It is designed as an enabler to create and process any kind of file or document in practice so far in current times or even could-be created in future times with unbelievably infinite memory limits. It provides limitless memory, file storage, screen timing and many more innovative limitless features and facilities. It has a unique memory mechanism, which integratingly keeps on multiplying & expanding itself to satisfy the needs of the user without creating any burden for the hardware and operating platform.

Time limits criteria for reels are burden of gone days. If required, ∀ breakdown a video in multiples and make multiple chains of reels, without losing any bit of content. And the beauty of that feature is that it flows smoothly without any jerk from current reel to the next reel. Another highlight is that the user can skip any particular portions of the reel-chain and can enjoy watching the favorite chunks as many as times.

Similarly, videos of any time-length can be created. The videos can have layers of many other videos. Pictures, videos, Games, films, TV Programmes, online classes, online meetings, live aired mobile, TV, OTT Shows or anything could-be watched in 3D Format in $\forall$.

It can create AI powered subtitles in videos in language of user's choice that also comes with variety of graphics, emojis and highlighters. It translates subtitles and audio content into any other language of another watcher in their respective devices. The videos created by $\forall$ or any other app, are smoothly playable in any kind of gadgets from variety of mobile applications, tabs, laptops, palm tops, desk tops, TV Screens etc.

$\forall$ provide live meets with no time limits and no limit on no's of participants. The smart features were in built language translator, sub-title language translator, real time recording & default archiving. At the same time its AI & CI enabled software act as muter to obscene or unparliamentary conversations or behavior at any point of time with real time effect.

$\forall$ Enables the user for any kind of e-commerce applications including safe payments which are compliant with PCI/DSS regulations.

Users can instruct $\forall$ for any kind of task, even if their language is imperfect. $\forall$ It is corrected through AI, CI, and electroencephalography.

One of the most astonishing aspects was that anything you want can be get done on verbal instructions too. That also not necessarily in the well-defined languages, but, in informal way of human language of daily life.

Even the user can listen any written content like the text messages, reviews, comments, and subtitles anywhere by selecting option 'Add Listen.'

The name of that miraculous app is 'ALL,' in use as a symbol ∀.

Likes, shares and comments flooded the infinite domain within few minutes. Seems that this reel could-be the fastest viraled content of recent times.

Few comments, recommendations and reciprocating comments as replies were really not-to-be-missed types, even more than the reel itself...

∀ **Bheja fry**

- Is it a song or puzzle? Asking God silly childish stuff.

∀ **Bigul**

- Hey buddy! It's a child only. See the face and listen to the voice; it's hardly 4 or 5 years old. But confusing, girl or boy?

∀ **FEMA**

- It's girl only. Watch body language and speaking style, which are just like those of girls only.

∀ **Style Mastro**

- I can read the persona; it's a girl only.

∀ **solo**

- Whatever, boy or girl? It doesn't matter. Just see the content, the song, lyrics, singing, everything seems naïve innocent and undoubtedly a new style of interacting with God

∀ **Bheja fry**

- Whatever, bro, but the idea of calling God that way could not be acceptable to me and maybe many more like me

∀ **solo**

- Listen to the song & read the subtitles again, bro...she is saying, "My mom and dad pray you, but I don't! I just love you. Do you love me too? This means it's crystal clear the child is in love with God. What else do you expect from a child who learns to love God?"

Meanwhile, many more likes & comments were continuously pouring in; a few comments were generic, a few were passive, and others were genuinely pulling attention from worldwide domains. Whatever was going on was proving again and again that the technical richness of any app can't guarantee enriching the class of social media responses.

∀ **Music lover**

- Hi! The background music selected is proof of innocence; it's like soothing devotional music.

∀ **heart**

- The content of the song is appealing. The child captured the chronology of her life sequentially very well. By her body language, she seemed an especially abled child, maybe autistic...

∀ **bolo**

- Yes, I also guess the same: the baby girl suffering from autism. That's why asking God, *"Hi God! Why was I born abnormal?"* If carefully watched, one can see that the child has never ever stood straight or perpendicular to the ground; throughout the video stood in slant positions, either bent on the right side or left side, or front side or backward.

∀ **Anything**

- But I doubt that it's autism. See the fluency of her oratory. It's without any irregular nodes. Though the voice is not clear, you know that such small children only talk in that way.

∀ Insane

- No, no, no. Don't jump the gun. If it is not clear, watch the video one more time rather than multiple times. It's not edited. It's directly shot in one go. There is no post-shoot dubbing. The song was originally sung in the original voice and has been retained. See, in between, the child is suffering spewing intermittently. Maybe it is out of her health condition or being especially abled.

∀ Solo Nome

- Bro, insane is right. Don't jump the guns. But I disagree that the singing is smooth. It's natural, but the voice is indistinctive and broken in many places. Watch carefully!

∀ Nodes

- Ya, it's not autism. See her body language, facial expressions, and voice culture. Though eyes seem to be under some intoxication, it is definitely not true because it's a 5 or 6-year-old girl. And no parent will allow any kind of intoxication to their child and make a video out of such a sorry condition. It's something else; maybe some doctor can understand and enlighten. But touched by the words she sang.

∀ rider

- As the girl is coughing and spewing intermittently, I doubt might be suffering from asthma, or maybe similar respiratory complications or maybe some indigestion disorders.

∀ poet planet

- Guys, I only see the lyrics in it because I am a poet. See, there are 9 paras, which are very well-sequenced if written by her own parents or maybe her own words. It's difficult to judge who is the creator of the lyrics is. A small child, especially an abled child, can't create such beautiful poetry where each part has some innovative content. However, one has to ignore grammar mistakes.

The very first para, *"Hi God! How are you? I am not well; how do you do?"* I have never had thoughts like this in my life, though I am a deeply religious person. It gives the very first clue about the mental condition of the child; she is trying to talk to God as if God is like a normal person around her in her day-to-day life.

Then openly said, "My Mom & Dad always pray *you. But I don't! I just love you! Do you love me too?"* This means that her parents are very religious persons who regularly pray to God or worship God. But, upfront, she says that she doesn't pray to God. Why? Reasons not told! Then, she throws another surprise by saying that she just loves God and inquisitively asks whether God also love her the same way or not. That shows childish immaturity and how sometimes children carry the teachings practically as per their innocent IQ levels.

In the third part, she is telling that she understands that God is the greatest entity in the universe. But, that status-quo of God can't stop her from asking necessary questions, keeping annoying her.

Then, in the fourth paragraph, her annoyance began simmering. Asked God, why was I born abnormal? The hidden question is, what is her fault? What is her parent's fault? Why is she destined for such a poor health condition? Her adamancy then explodes into sarcasm, asking further whether her condition is acceptable to God or if it's a new normal for him. And whether she will also have to accept this specially-abled condition as a new normal in her existence with no choice.

I know my response is dragging beyond tolerance but let me complete it. Please bear with me in the interest of good wishes to this mysterious girl child, singing a peculiar song going viral in the latest record-breaking scales.

Let's leave the fifth para; it's a normal thing. In the sixth & seventh para, she shares her emotions about being the lone child of the family, and children from neighborhoods refrain from playing with her. So, requesting God to be her brother or sister and to play with her. Doesn't it sound so emotional to a child, even if it's an abnormal one?

In the eighth stanza, she is further inquisitive and keeps on asking what exactly is lying in God's mind and cautioning not to be unresponsive, acting as deaf, dumb, or blind. A person who is deeply in irrecoverable troubles can only be such blunt mouth while interfacing with God.

When we matured persons don't know, can't guess when God could respond to our prayers, worships, questions, then what emotions we can expect from toddlers. In the last verse, she behaves as talking to someone in real-life, counting numbers while expecting God to respond. But when found no response, then innocently request God to call back when get free...Ha ha ha, that's the height of childish innocence...

Every saying in this video touched my heart. All the good wishes and blessings to the girl, let God save her and bless her with normal fulfilling life.

Thanks for your patience.

∀ **man-to-man**

- What the hell is this? That is such a long comment. Kudos to this app, which allows such larger-than-sky comments, whereas no other app allows such junk. One can also express it in a few words.

∀ **gyan**

- People like Poetplanet don't leave any opportunity to milk any undue disadvantage of facilities provided by any app. Ridiculous, shameful....

∀ **poetplanet**

- Dear ∀ man to man, I already conveyed my gratitude, so why such hue and cry? After all, I wrote this large chunk only in the interest of supporting that child. I didn't do anything wrong by explaining in detail so that people can understand from a poet's point of view and perspective of expressions through poetry.

∀ **man-to-man**

- Bro, pardon me. I can't take anymore. Think about others also; many might get irritated by your boring chunks. God bless you.

∀ Poet planet smelled the filth and didn't respond. Meanwhile, a lot of comments were being showered, like cats and dogs, with a few criticisms and a few praises. On the darker side of social media platforms, one can be trolled for its good as well as bad expressions in public domains. Your good may be bad for many, and your bad may be good for many. Because, more than genuine users, social media harvested uncountable trollers, who are not self-driven but often paid entities, serving the vested interests of many shady hypocrites.

Though global leaders with noble intentions designed democracy as best long-term way of sociology, where freedom of expressions and criticism were glorified as essential elements of democracy.

'Freedom of expression' empowers every single person down the line in society to come forward to express their concerns bothering about their existences.

And 'criticism' to find, analyse and highlight the pros & cons of any phenomenon in any walk of life, with prudent solutions for continual and inclusive improvements in society.

But of late, people or groups of people carrying one-sided vested interests intentionally misused 'freedom of expression' to dent the social fabric in their own favor.

They misused 'criticism,' either as a tool kit to harm competitor or rivals or to vent out their own frustration born out of their own flaws & incompetencies.

Similar unhealthy trends of 'freedom of expression' and 'criticism' have also been observed in such naïve videos, where such a small, innocent, specially-abled girl child showcases her love for God in her own childish way.

However the video crossed million marks within couple of hours and billion marks in couple of days, making it the record-breaking content in recent days and the overnight internet sensation across the globe.

A graph of curiosity was rising against the law of motion to know about the girl child who became SHERO, surpassing all existing public figures and celebrities.

Meanwhile, a few comments escalated the sensations...

∀ **dr100**

- Generally, I am not active on social media, but I couldn't stop this time after watching the emotional content created by a toddler. Being a doctor, I feel that the child should treat her abnormality. The video couldn't hint previously about the nature of the abnormality. I would like to help the parents without any financial burden. If somebody can find out the contact details of the girl child, please let me know.

Immediately, the doctor got a lot of praise from all-around but was unable to locate the child. A few more doctors across the globe came forward gracefully and expressed their gratitude to help the child.

A few well-known stalwart business tycoons also responded, wishing to help the child.

A few NGOs also expressed their willingness to help the child.

Politicians and proud political workers just saw the reel, passively posted likes, and continued being busy in their day-to-day offline and online mudslinging.

So-called stalwarts from the entertainment industries watched multiple times, hesitantly postponed submitting their likes, but started the process of milking that unique way of calling

God. But, cautiously enough, they also burnt their fingers in a few films, stage performances, Ott contents, TV serials, and music videos, where God was portrayed in an illicitly humorous way and strong public arrogant reactions flopped those projects. Even regulatory bodies and judiciary also discontinued supporting such contents, where Gods have been abused, and faiths have been hurt. So, the masterminds started thinking with an innovative, harmless approach because they sensed it was an excellent money-churning idea if it worked smartly.

Media, especially News channels, also didn't remain untouched. The business compulsions of TRP compelled them to showcase this viral video as breaking news with as much time as possible space. In addition to that, they started airing debate programs centered on the essence of the cult video.

But as we know, good and bad co-exist irrespective of time zones. Few perverts couldn't stop their venom from trying to pollute the harmony of such harmonious social media...

∀ **up down**

- All rubbish. Don't get carried away by artificial emotions cunningly created by using the innocence of a minor. It's all to divert people's minds from real necessary issues bothering societies all across the nation and even all across the globe.

∀ **My God is great**

- What filth all-around? Mindless people like this insane video. It's demeaning God. How can someone address God disrespectfully like this? It's not less than blasphemy. The girl seems like a demon, insulting God. Must be punished.

∀ **Not gyan**

- I condemn this craziness. It will fuel the fire lit by radicals and even by atheists who want to make this world God-free.

As many people say, nobody can control freedom of expression in this pseudo democratic society. Everybody can't be pleased in this conveniently secular world. Whatever, but the majority of the posted billion views, comments, and likes were indicating supporting and praising the girl child for her innocent, unprofessional natural singing talent, and the innovative flavours of the content...

The video is trending not only on ∀ but also on all existing social media apps. The innovatively powerful specs of ∀ transported the video on all other social media apps in real time, and they were also being flooded with all-around kudos.

Wise people could understand the reasons behind the success of that video.

First and foremost the overall aura being created by the unique persona, body language and the raw childish singing of the baby girl.

The angelic face of the child looked like a reincarnation of innocence in the best human form.

Her sky-blue eyes looked intoxicated throughout the video, in each frame, in each close-up. Her eye movements were inconsistent and unpredictable. The eye-apples rolling here and there uncontrollably, irrespective of the essence of the lyrics.

Her blonde hairs, scattered over forehead and kissing eyebrows, hanging behind hugging the shoulders, seemed as naturally combed, waving with rhythm of soothing winds around.

The glimpses of her overall body movements, reasoning inquisitiveness towards the status-quo of her health, but without any clear picture. Leg movements, shaking of hands, and facial nodes are also asking the same questions.

Though many noted and commented that the girl sang the song in a natural, cute, childish voice at a higher pitch & a slower speed, with a little bit of control over dynamic changes of voice, somehow managing her voice tone, and little bit succeeded in expressing vivid emotions as per the mood of the lyrics. The whole singing did flow seamlessly, in appreciable sync of melody, voice, tone and expressions, except for a couple of natural hiccups where she gestured as coughing & spewing. Her willingness and control over singing, despite some physical disturbance, made people shower praises on her.

Overall it was a delight to watch a pleasant content with innovative ideas presented in unique way by an especially abled girl child conveying sense of food for thoughts.

A unique internet content, sympathy for the presenter and curiosity for the secret behind the presenter's health issue were the salient pointers of that reel...

Many expressed thanks to ∀ to showcase such soulful content, which, as per them, served as food for thought and reasons to think further about relations between humans and God...

Chapter 2

Hi God! How are you?

Second Reel - Especially Abled

03rd December

Fairy posted her 2nd **reel on** ∀.

Hi God! How are you?
I am not fine, what about you?
Why I born like especially abled children?
It give me feel like being stepchildren...
Thousands born every day, not all fairly survive.
Few die untimely as infant, few before five.
Tears of those mothers never get dry,
Do you console them, or, you silently cry.
Like me, few born with lifetime disorder,
Is it KARMA, or, sometimes you are out of order?
They live like half-life & half-death,
Is it fair anyway, or, you enjoy the feath?
And those who survive, not all get fair nurture,
Few struggle always in thirst and hunger.
All these sore truths rising my anger,
Come on God! Say something loud and clear,
If you also get especially abled child like us,
What you will feel and do, honestly tell us.
I will be waiting for you,
Take your time, I won't disturb you...

∀ **first**

- Wow! After long time *"Hi God! How are you?"* Good going this time too, but why so late?

The very first response flashed within a fraction of a second when this reel was posted by that mysterious baby girl. Soon, responses as comments, counter comments, likes & shares started flowing faster than anything in the cosmos.

∀ **Lolol**

- Ya! The mystery babes is back. Nice song this time again. But why a long gap? Almost one year…

∀ **awake**

- No, dear! It's not a long gap. The baby doll posted many reels in between, but those were very short, hardly 2-3 seconds, yelling only "Hi God! How are you?" Maybe that's why it didn't attract an audience; I don't understand why?

∀ **solo**

- Boss! Who is interested in 2-3 seconds of half-cooked stuff? But after a long gap, it seems to be thought-provoking content again. Listen and read each and every word and line carefully…Feel more sentimental this time.

∀ **ilu**

- But how? A child can't create such a deeply thoughtful song; it's definitely guided by her parents or somebody else.

The unstoppable huge flow of responses – comments, likes & shares were reaching beyond human control, which to be read or left. But then the extraordinarily designed AI & CI quickly started filtering and prioritizing with highlighters for the deserving comments found with unmatchable X-factor by merit or the other way round also.

∀ **virus**

- Folks, I like this. Again, few never seen before punches. The second verse shook my heart – *"Why I born like especially abled children? It makes me feel like being stepchildren…"*

The girl spilt bitter reality. Let me share my personal experience. There are 3 children in our family. My youngest brother is an especially abled child. Our family takes great care of him, but despite all the goodness, I don't know why he often complains about being treated like a step-child. I don't know from where he gets such negative vibes and why? But it's very difficult for such a child and their family to keep an unchallengeable balance in their pitied life.

∀ **med**

- Absolutely right. I am a medical professional and have spent my whole life in this field. Attended a lot of such cases and helped a lot of children grow gracefully without making them feel like somebody deprived. But any amount of caring and love sometimes fails, too, when suddenly such children break out with emotional outbursts highlighting their being something inferiorly different from the so-called normal people. Surprisingly, mostly, they don't express such feelings every now and then, but deep inside their heart and subconscious minds, the thought of being disabled but selectively tagged as especially abled irritates them a lot.

∀ **I'm Still Great**

- Guys! I hope everybody can find me one of the best living examples of this issue.

Before that guy could have continued after the coincidental break of the one-liner and posted further, many, many reactions started raining, like cats and dogs intermittently welcoming with tonnes of welcoming appreciation.

As a renowned global celebrity ∀, ImstillGreat was popularly known as one of the all-time great examples from a family of especially abled people. This guy hailing from the USA was born without arms & legs out of an extremely rare congenital disorder known as Phocomelia.

I struggled like in hell mentally, physically, and emotionally, and was bullied at school in pre-nursery, nursery, and primary school classes. Later, he was compelled circumstantially to drop out of the conventional school. But he didn't allow the cruel Nature to further damage his reactive aspirations, which were born out of unavoidable frustrations and the urge to prove himself in front of the human world of biased, convenient, preferential expressions.

Later, after overcoming the worldly taboos, ∀ImstillGreat won many Paralympic tournaments for various ranges of sports. Additionally, as a freelancer performer, I set records for many other international activities like being the sole diver for intercontinental sea channels, mountaineering at Everest, sky diving, running the longest road in the world, paragliding, sky diving, etc. He was one of the most greatly blessed guys in the world who was absolutely loved by everyone, not a single hater existing currently, and 'zero' trollers for his social media & offline presence.

But people are people. Their sentiments are always on roller coaster clouds ascending or descending. Always to be loved, respected, and accommodated. But, this time, the only surprising scenario was that everybody reacted positively, praising ∀ImstillGreat by all means and further requesting to bless this girl child directly or with a few motivational tips.

Though the storm of reactions didn't seem to be settling down, somehow the great living legend as ever gracefully struggling, managed somehow, and posted in continuation of his earlier one-liner reaction.

∀ **ImstillGreat**

- Oh my God! I have no words for such a huge tsunami of love for me. But I feel to divert this tsunami of love towards ∀ Fairy....She needs it most right now...genuinely....Am I right? I think all my well-wishers will agree with me.

BTW, based on my own life journey and experience, I feel that any especially abled child shouldn't be subjected to any kind of apathy in any condition. Parents, family, relatives, near & dear ones, neighbors, doctors, teachers, colleagues, and anybody coming across shouldn't allow any kind of apathy towards the especially born child. Rather, they should sense and religiously practice empathy for the so-called so understood child without exhibiting any clue of sympathising with them.

Often, your supportive actions and your caring, if otherwise felt by the child as intentional & well-planned sympathy, may derail the process of helping.

So guys, you must believe me, it's a unique kind of very delicate issue. How to handle the psyche of especially abled children. It's not only physical or emotional or mental but beyond the mathematical equations of probabilities, permutations & combinations. The more exposure and more understanding of the contrast between the normal and abnormal ignites the emotional turbulence to the tune of suicidal wishes.

So, the world needs to get educated for the normalisation of body language, behavioral science, facial expressions, eye's expressions and even control over tongue whenever coming across any especially abled people, either planned or suddenly.

Watching Fairy singing "Hi God! How are you?" in an indistinctive, stuttering baby voice, wearing a naively innocent face and seeming like intoxicated eyes while spewing intermittently, shook my heart more than any terrible tremor. As I was unable to guess what exactly she was suffering from, it made me so emotional. It reminded me of my own life journey and compelled me to help her with anything she needed at any point of time.

Though you all call me the Bravo Warrior, but after all we are human and now I am feeling unable to control my tears.

I just want to say, dear ∀ Fairy! Look at me!! We are not disabled or especially abled or differently abled, but more abled than ordinary people.

We can do whatever ordinary people can do, but they can't do whatever wonders we can do...Please remember my these words.

Never ever feel pity on yourself, never ever feel like being step-child. We are not ordinary child, but reincarnation of God itself.

Forget everything, forget about yourself, just keep on singing as much as possible....You are a uniquely great singer. I do hope and bless that one day, you will become the top singer in the world.

Hi Fairy! Please don't hesitate and knock me any time you need any help!! I will be waiting for your call.....see you, bye, bye.....

∀ **Imstill** Great not only posted this soulful narrative but ornamented it with video orating the same narration being displayed as subtitles.

∀ **Imstill** Great's emotional posts stole many hearts. Many genuine and reactive posts followed later in much larger volumes.

Other social media channels also got flooded with responses, breaking their earlier records.

Meanwhile a post flashed in between by ∀ poetplanet, who was badly trolled last time long ago when ∀ Fairy posted her debut post.

∀ **poetplanet**

- I swore last time not to be active again on social media, but such a deeply emotional reel from ∀ Fairy made me to come back. But guys, don't worry. This time, I am not going to irritate you guys with an intolerable long post, but I will share my points in tolerable bits and pieces.

As soon as the post appeared, the troll army jumped in with the best possible hate words and seemed to be trying their level best to demoralise ∀ poetplanet to continue further in this series of responses against the second reel of ∀ Fairy.

∀ **axe**

- No no…not again. Dear poet! I am ready to pay any price. Please don't pollute the ambience of Fairy's reel.

∀ **$$$**

- Ready to throw any bounty to keep ∀ poetplanet away from this wonderful baby girl

And many more gentle and naughty trolls flooded this time. But the adamant ∀ poetplanet seemed to be trying to show off as troll-proof social media-savvy.

∀ **poetplanet**

- No comments for verse 1, as it is generic. Absolutely agree with ∀ ImstillGreat and others for verse 2.

Verse 3 is quite serious, when it comes from the heart of a minor. I don't know from where she gets educated about this issue and how gets all these sensitive information, which are highlighting the infant survival rates.

Anybody can check from WHO, UNO, DATA, or OGD India that the survival rate of newborns is declining over time. Those who survive are not fortunate enough; many still live under various life-threatening factors till attaining the age of 5 years.

WHO, UNO, Medical Fraternity all over the world, the Health Ministry of India and all other countries in the world are well aware of this paining serious issue. All The facts & figures continue to update about the efforts being put for R & D to combat such pathetic life loss, but nothing significant has been done so far.

Still, every now and then, we get NEWS about mysterious deaths of newborns and minors for known & unknown inexplicable reasons.

Where science is failing, or where governance & administration are failing? Nobody honestly comes forward to take responsibility or to define the accountability.

Whenever such heart-wrenching incidents come into the public domain, the only reactions from the undefined responsible or accountable people are often found as if intended for quick eye wash to the scenario using their proven managerial tactics.

Will God listen to ∀Fairy or not, we can't predict. But can hope that government leaders, medical & health industry leaders of entire world, WHO, UNO must listen to the saddened voice of people through this baby Fairy….

Today's age is the age of quickies and shorties. Nobody is interested in lingering slow and lengthy content of any nature, specifically if it is some sort of passive wisdom.

More than that, the language often used in social media chats is not in clean or gentle forms but in vaguely slang grammarless form as in spoken languages. Lately, however, it has been felt that the use of AI-enabled Chat GPT and other similar applications reformed the contemporary social media practice of using unpleasant language. Though still, one can see slang indelicate grammarless languages in chats in many other old apps; surprisingly, it ∀ set a great example with its clean content as far as the dignity of chat content amid the existing image of insolent behavioral patterns of social media nerds.

So, despite a valuable response from ∀poetplanet, it again failed to earn any accolades from troller tribes. But there were positive responses as well from many who seemed to have gone through the pains of questionable survival rates of infants or minors. They even throw slaps on trollers who exhibited insensitivity towards such a delicately emotional issue hurting humanity.

And there, the controversial poet again posted a heart-wrenching post.

∀ **poetplanet**

- Thanks for the positive views from good souls and wishing for troller evils for a long, peaceful life. Now, coming to verse 4, nothing could be more emotional beyond the tears of a mother. Who carries and nurtures one more life inside her body for 9 months. Later, when the time comes to deliver that life into this world, and if she is told that the holy piece of her body couldn't see the light of this world. There are no words in this human world to narrate the specific or array of emotions she goes through.

Wise literates and medical professionals narrated such scenarios in their own words, wrapped under their own wisdom and experiences, but nothing could weigh or measure the pain of that mother's tears who lost her just-born child.

I was surprised to see an escalation of such an issue after a long, long time, that also not by someone adult from any walk of life, but, from a minor girl child.

Thanks to her, thanks to her parents, who somehow remind society to raise their voices against still existing newborn fatalities under suspicious excuses.

I could guess that when not getting any true answer from society, Fairy decided to ask the God. What is God's response to any incident of newborn death? Does God console the suffering mother? Or does God cry secretly in silence?

Most people agree that I never ever saw anybody asking silly stuff that way to someone or even to God.

Here, atheists aren't on the radar, but only those who, either way, believe in any form of God.

But I am surprised! Who can ask such questions to God? Either a wise person with unmatchable IQ, EQ & SQ, or someone who literally lacks in IQ, EQ & SQ, or a spineless, careless atheist. But this child doesn't seem belonging to any of these categories. Ultimately she is creating her own tribe, who doesn't worship God traditionally, but loves God, and talks to God as like talking to own close buddy.

Many reactions followed praising ∀poetplanet for so heart touching opinion as comments, likes, and shares. But addicted trollers remained confirmed slaves of their negating habits, even for such emotional truth.

One popular golden words, Good & Bad exist together. Good can survive without Bad, but Bad can't survive without Good. It seems true when trollers throw their tantrums hoping to hurt the ∀poet planet, but the other way around, they expose themselves further.

∀ **kudos**

- Guys, this is not any poet. A poet can say a thousand words or a long story in just a few words.

∀ **whistle**

- Right bro. It's a duck.

∀ **f0c0k**

- Why not the app admin fu...k off this parroty?

Many didn't like such demeaning reactions and hit back. Even ∀poetplanet couldn't control and shot a shocker.

∀ **poetplanet**

- Bro! I am an author, too. A content writer, too. So, mind your business before spewing any dirt.

But trollers are trollers, thick-skinned and perverts, either playing their own self or driven by their shady pay masters using social media as a tool kit for maintaining their autocratic supremacy in virtual worlds, too...

Meanwhile, another post by ∀ poetplanet flashed in continuity...

∀ **poetplanet**

Perplexed when I heard, "Like me, few are born with lifetime disorder. Is *it KARMA, or sometimes you are out of order?"* I couldn't understand at first glance what the hell she was trying to say? Initially, no words came to my mind for this inquisitively challenging quest.

I feel sad when she says that there are few unfortunate children who are born with birth defects as lifetime disorders, still incurable by modern medical science. Mainly severe congenital disorders, which, despite all preventive pre-natal measures, couldn't be diagnosed, and then the inability of medical science for quick-fix or permanent cure.

But once when a child is born with such birth defects, the medical fraternity starts justifying reasons out of known scientific expertise or even guesswork as open-ended R & D. But, see the psyche of this suffering baby girl, who is naively asking God if her birth defect is the result of any so-called KARMA? Maybe it was from her parents or her own previous life. Though God is God and remains silent always, even humans couldn't answer truthfully.

And then orates one of the weirdest verbal punches I have ever heard in my life, "*or, sometimes you are out of order?"* In my weirdest nightmares, I feel that nobody, even an atheist, also couldn't express their displeasure by addressing God that way. Are you out of order sometimes, resulting in such cruel pain to an innocent little bundle of joy?

With every next verse, the quest of this mystery Fairy unfolds new expressions for one's relation with God.

As usual, this post also got accolades from sensible and brickbats from senseless geeks.

But this micro-celebrity continued with another post in continuation....

∀ **poetplanet**

- In the sixth verse, she further knocks God by saying that such children like her with severe incurable birth defects are always compelled to live in a miserable way, like neither alive nor dead. Those pains can be felt by those only who are facing half-life & half-death situations or by their biological near & dear ones. Doctors are seen as experimenting their best only, and others are seen as passive witnesses.

But, then she asks God, are such odds fair by any means?

Or does God enjoy keeping people in such a state of neither life nor death?

On the one hand, the questions appear stupid, childish, immature, and a waste of time. But, if we look into it from beyond the horizons of orthodox doctrines, there is no harm in exploring answers to such rare quests maybe something helpful scientific solution could come out, which can better the lives of future generations against such congenital disorders.

Again, I don't know whether God has any answers different from what our scriptures & wise have taught us since millenniums. But we, the current generation must set this as ethical responsibility to work out some doable solution to prevent such painful births in future, or, even if it happens, then full proof solutions to cure the stubborn incurables.

Again, many likes, shares and comments flooded in response to this deeply emotional expression where the majority of geeks were sympathetic but non-conclusive. Whereas the troll army again pelted stones by maligning the comments as illogical stuff.

And their accolades were booming like anything for ∀ Fairy. But the troll army kept on poking with their filth.

After a few hours, the most loved and most hated guy again posted a concluding narrative.

∀ **poetplanet**

- Guys! Now, I am concluding my take by combining the rest of the verses from the seventh to the tenth. Further, Fairy keeps on saying that even after surviving death, not all those unfortunate children get a fair upbringing, and many face malnutrition. I think that although the UNO, WHO, and governments all might be working seriously on this part of life, it seems that it's not enough. In addition to that, societies across the world must listen to her and must extend their best possible help to such children.

Then she expressed her anger for this whole issue and asked God to speak out about a child's emotions…

Then suddenly, she asks, if an especially abled child like her is born in their own family, what will God feel and do to heal their own child? Such unusual thoughts….only a child can think and can ask to God….

Finally, I request everybody who comes across Fairy and children like her to please support them with the best possible help. Let them mingle fairly in normal society and practice the same life courses as normal people.

Though ∀poetplanet said bid adieu, but, the social media domain, as usual, never ever took a rest and kept on flowing uncontrollably. There were so many think tanks, commenters, and chatters like ∀poetplanet that seemed to be competing or chatting like group discussions in rapidly prolonging threads.

And there Fairy was watching her own reel, sitting in the laps of her mom and dad…..

CHAPTER 3

Third Reel - Business Of Birth Rights

03rd December

Fairy posted her 3rd reel on ∀.

Hi God! How are you?
I am not happy, what about you?
They debarred me from school,
Its sad, to miss the knowledge pool.
Why many children like me not allowed by the rule?
Say something, now I am losing my cool...
I am not alone, who is troubled,
Many children alike are in this world.
Reasons are many more, serious & catchy,
Unhealthiness, poverty, backwardness, anarchy...
And they say, education is every child's birth right,
Then why it became a business, and, fees are so high.
They also say, health care is every child's birth right,
Then why it became a business, and, costs are so high.
Humanity needs free education & free health care for all the children,
If world want to see wise and healthy generations.
Rulers promise every now and then,
Unable to ensure, it will happen when?
Think for us God! Show some light,
Take away darkness, make our life bright...

After one year, Fairy appeared again with her next reel, which had a few more children-specific sensitive issues.

This time brimming, Fairy looked more upset while chanting her emotional quest for birthright to education & health for children. Her fans couldn't gulp her tears and responded uncanny.

∀ **baby globe**

- Kudos! What a wonderful reel again! This time, Fairy is asking God for Fair education & health for every child, which is also free. Good thoughts, dear.....

∀ **smile**

- This time, I couldn't tolerate her tears. Why that school debarred her? It is an unpardonable act by any school if they treat especially abled children in an inhuman way. Fairy and her parents must lodge a police complaint against the school and must approach the Court for justice.

∀ **babe care**

- It's really a pity in this new modern world when the majority of the population is open-minded about accommodating the underprivileged. Shaming incidents keep on taking place every now & then despite society's tall claims of absolute equality.

"Save the Girl Child, Educate the Girl Child" are slogans popularised by political leaders and governments; even though efforts are in place, they are not adequate enough. Lot more to be done. If the system fails to take care of such cases as Fairy, society's common people need to come forward to help out the suffering children.

Please DM to join me to run a social media movement for helping Fairy to get admission in the school.

The initiative taken by ∀ baby care was responded to very well by positive-minded nerds but, at the same time, criticized by the troll army.

∀ **who cares**

- Guys! Don't be emotional fools. It has almost been more than 2 years. Does anybody have any idea about the whereabouts of Fairy? Beware! It could-be scam too. Check her profile, its locked. She is enjoying having record-breaking strength of followers, but surprisingly not following anybody.

∀ **careless**

- You are right, Bro! She is selling tears just to earn sympathy.

∀ **junky**

- Not only earning sympathy. She is sure shot earning huge amounts of dollars as well. Nobody knows who she is & where she is. However, this app ∀ must know her very well in order to disburse the earnings. If money fails to help her in getting retained in that school, why don't the app owners come forward to help her out?

∀ **badas**

- Because the app owner could also be a partner in this scam. But, you know, often people love to be cheated by such scammers.

The hatred thread was dragging beyond irritations, then suddenly a Fairy fan dropped a soft bomb…

∀ **roses**

- Enough is enough. All app owners must remove all these perverts and ban them immediately. These guys are not a social media troll army but inhuman and scammers themselves.

Mind your business; innocents don't sell tears. You naked illiterates are selling your filth. It will take ages for you to understand the emotions of sufferers. Better, you people shut your mouth and don't pollute the holy virtual environment around Fairy.

One troller responded quickly…

∀ **pothole**

- Bro! We have no sympathy for a brain-blind like you. Future will tell soon, who is selling what?

Before that blunt reaction was responded, the well-known poetplanet jumped into the pool.

∀ **poetplanet**

- Reminding golden words. GOOD can live without BAD, but BAD can't live without GOOD.

- So beware parasites....I mean, troll guerrilla army! You spineless aliens are surviving not on your own but on the virtual blood of Fairy and good souls like us.

Jokes apart, again, I couldn't restrain myself after watching one more emotional piece of dialogue with God. Don't worry, dear troll army; this time, I will make it fairly brief.

Fairy seemed as sad after getting expelled from the school, though specific details are not there. The reason is already known to us, as she is an especially abled child. But there are dedicated schools for such children. Her parents must take her there. Why don't they act that way? Not clear. As her personal details are still unknown, it's very difficult for us to help her out. The question will remain open-ended....

Yes, there are many children like her.

Despite all the wholesome awareness across the globe, there are still many unfortunate children who are underprivileged as far as fair education and fair health are concerned. There are many reasons for this, but precise solutions are missing, as usual.

Leaders are always agree for education & health as birth right of each child but lacks in ensuring fair implementation without any financial constraint.

The modern age policies for child education & health are to be reviewed further along with the current business models in practice.

Better try to implement India's systems of child education & health care practices of pre-invasion periods where education and child health care were not money-minting businesses but selfless services by the current generation for the next generations.

Unfortunately in today's world, child education and child health care are modelled like corporate business by money minded society leaders to fetch vested interests of own self & allies.

The humanity element is missing for both basic needs of children, and still, we claim & expect a bright future for coming generations. How come it will happen, nobody is having any full proof idea.

So finally, Fairy requests God to look into these matters, to dispel the darkness, to bring light into their lives...Can God do any favor to Fairy or not? Future only can tell...

In my opinion, we shouldn't judge and react from our own individual perspective but from the perspective of a child, specifically from an especially abled child. How do new-age children look into issues affecting them and their thought processes, and how do they react to their childish expectations?

BTW it's not a traditional virtual review but a tribute to dear Fairy...

This time, the poetplanet seemed a little bit aggressive and couldn't meet the commitment for comparatively smaller content. Promised for a brief response, but, again, it was huge actually. And as taunted in the initial phase of comments, the troll army quickly fired tonnes of ammunition.

∀ **menotrollmepolice**

- If that's the size of a fairly brief, then I doubt the meaning of brief. The word 'brief' might need redefining.

It's true that Fairy is a child, and one should understand her childish psyche & expressions. But I smell that she is not any ordinary, but a mystery girl child who is being driven by cunning hidden souls in the background.

But it's a pity when a mature poet mumbles childishly.

What's your problem with the current education system and health care system?

If you provide free education for all, then how will you pay the salaries of teachers & staff?

If you provide free health care for all, then how you will pay salary of doctors and medical staff and how will you buy hospital equipments, medicines, other consumables, etc.

BTW, you must know that still, in a lot of demographies, education is free for girls, children below the poverty line, and in a few government sectors, PSU and charity institutions.

Still, health care is free for employees and their families in PSUs, a few government organisations, and charity hospitals. Even free health insurance is there for people below the poverty line and for people having low per-capita income.

If you want free education and free health care for children of the entire nation, then how will you manage the finances to run the education & health organisations? In today's world, these have not remained as community service like in the pre-invasion era but as money-generating industries and being run like corporate companies.

So, it could-be suicidal to change the system overnight or even in phases.

Better to continue with the existing education systems with necessary well-defined, agreeable amendments of fee structures in those so-called costly private schools and colleges by making subsidised affordable fee structures. There could-be standard fee structure for pan-nation locations. Again that should be as per services cum facility parameters of different grades or economic levels of institutions.

Similarly, for health care services, standardization of prices and rates could-be done by matching with demographies and suiting to current per-capita incomes.

See off late how the huge price differences in generic and trendy medicines have been handled and affordability enabled for the masses. Similarly, the cost of other parts of treatments could be made affordable.

It's true that education & health care are the birthright of every child, but that doesn't mean that we should suppress the institutions that are managing to run these community services even as businesses.

You must know that in the past, a few countries went bankrupt who implemented free education and free health care along with many other services like free electricity, water, transportation, etc.

Freebee culture can provide short-lived temporary or contemporary comforts, but it will be suicidal in the long run.

Free culture will destroy people's ability and zeal to work to earn bread & butter.

Free culture was experimented on by a few national leaders in their countries as an appeasement tool to grab power and remain in power for a long. And that model of governance destroyed the DNA of those countries; right now, I can't remember the names of those countries….But you can find it on Google.

Similarly, in India, few political leaders are misguidedly alluring populations by practicing Freebee Culture as a silent appeasement tool for vote banks, just to grab power and to remain in power for long. Beware, such free culture political tantrums will not only harm the National Treasure but will gradually transform people's psyche as slackers addicted to everything as free. And then that will be more dangerous for coming generations either to continue as free suckers or to come out from free culture. Ultimately, in the near future, the nation will suffer in irreparable fragments.

Better we must educate & train people enabling them to earn and parallaly workout right price for their all-basic needs like education, health care, electricity, water, insurance, transportation etc.

Preaching is easy, but the right implementation and practice are very difficult.

So before opening mouth, one should work out 360^0, evaluate pros & cons prudently and then check the inclusive feasibility.

What the hell it was? The netizens were perplexed at such a giant reaction from troll police. Reacted in the same pattern as the huge write-up, point by point.

Soon, troll army warriors showered accolades on ∀ menotrollmepolice and, this time, even appreciated by a few others also who generally dislike & avoid such trollers.

Even poetplanet couldn't restrain from reacting...

∀ **poetplanet**

- Wow! For the first time in my life, I saw that trollers also sometimes have vigilant brains and sensible hearts, but the outcome is sheer in vain. Bro! Open your consciousness and try to understand that Free Health Care & Free Education for children can't be defined as a financial burden on the government but as a holistic investment towards the recurring betterment of the next generations.

History lauds that India was known as Vishwa guru toping the charts of literacy rate, wisdom, health, economic prosperity and many more parameters before the unfortunate barbaric invasions since sometimes thousand year back.

Historians expressed esteem and clarity regarding the reasons behind India's world leader status as inclusively prudent implementations of people-friendly policies and governance by contemporary rulers.

The right time will never ever come; the current ongoing time is always the right time to remove the spectacles of invaders and to assimilate our old education and healthcare systems to improve the quality of life of our future generations.

Threads of responses went on endlessly…..the reel kept on rising beyond past virality records…

And there the mystery Fairy was intermittently watching reactions and somehow surviving amid pains….

CHAPTER 4

Hi God! How are you?

<u>Fourth Reel - Issues Blues</u>

03rd December

Fairy posted her 4th reel.

Hi God! How are you?
I missed you a lot, did you miss me too?
    Dad says you made the world very nice & beautiful,
    But then why many lives are sad & dull...
I won't talk for those who are doing well and happy,
But, for those neglected poor sad and unhappy.
    Hi God! There are many endless paining issues,
    Rulers come & go, but problems still continue.
Since long why always there is inflation,
Rulers failed often, passing it to next generation.
    Since ages why often farmers do suicide,
    Why still a better life for them is denied.
Since ages why many often suffer starvation,
Full belly rulers often overlook their condition.
    Why often poor become poorer, and, rich become richer,
    Rulers always silent, can you reverse the picture.
Why every generation suffer unemployment,
Rulers promise tall, but often lead disappointment.
    How long there will be corruption, terrorism & crime,
    Rulers trying their best, but, when will fully decrime...
Why still rape and many crimes against women?
Laws & Rulers often failing, why don't you remodel men?
    Why no true control on pollution and global warming,

UNO and Rulers acting pseudo, can you counter the warning?
No control on over rising population, seems scary & lethal.
Human acting foolish in your name, please solve this riddle?
Time & again many act intolerant shaming ethics,
Law often helpless, to save the social basics...
Why often wars, spoiling peace and harmony?
UNO always useless, who will set the symphony?
Come on God! Answer my questions.
Before it's too late, take some actions.

After many summers & winters the cult words "Hi God! How are you" echoed virtually again in dopey voice from the mystery girl gazing into sky with her intoxicatingly sparkling eyes, walking tottered like a drunkard and wearing much grown-up angelic face attracting cosmos all-around.

Almost after a decade, a long reel came from Fairy.

Where in hibernation she had been and why? Nobody knew.

Earlier netizens enquired about Fairy on social media, but, in the absence of any reliable clue, with the passing of time, public memory faded as usual.

Meanwhile, as usual, the cosmos has changed a lot from Earth to Moon to Marsh to Galaxies.

The world on Earth changed a lot with the birth of many new demographies, countries, species, protagonists, antagonists, values, quotients, technologies, and economies.

The only thing that had not changed was "$\forall$" the king of apps, still reigning the global social media unanimously. The reasons were many, few genuine and few controversial.

Leaving controversies aside, many smiled when they saw that Fairy was back. And this time, she carried a little bit lengthier content but again found very close to the hearts and souls of the people. Though again unable to understand the psyche of that mystery girl, what prompted her to raise her voice for people centric issues? However, after all those years, she seemed like a grown-up teenager; many were of the opinion that age factor often matters in one's thought process and expressions.

As it often happened with her reels, this time also views, likes, shares and comments started pouring in and intermittently sometimes as cloud bursts...

Many comments earned kudos from like-minded social media animals but brickbats also from angry birds...

∀ **loyal dog**

- No words. What a content from now a teenager? How nicely interweaved almost all the social issues in a festoon. From inflation to farmer's issues to malnutrition to rich-poor gaps to unemployment to crime, corruption, terrorism to crime against women to global warming to overpopulation to rising intolerances to wars, global peace....almost all the contemporary social issues are addressed. Then, ask God to help out, as the current global ruler's pseudos can't solve the issues. God bless you, Fairy!

∀ **waves**

- Extremely right, Bro! But, in India, these are not problems only of the current age but have been cyclical problems since independence. One can say almost perennial. Inflation, unemployment, farmer's suicide, corruption, crime, atrocities against women, rich-poor gap, uncontrolled population growth....unfortunately, all these have been happening since our grandfather's period, if we count it since independence.

Global warming is the byproduct of the vaguely grown industrial revolution.

Terrorism evolved as the brainchild of narrow, shallow ideologies of supremacy hungry hollow leaders since many centuries and often troubling humanity like misguided missiles.

Time and again, history has proved that wars are not the right solutions to any conflict, but rather dialogues addressing dual sided concerns. But since ages, leaders have failed to avoid wars, and ultimately, wars became the right tool as the only solution for the survival of civilisations at the cost of extinction of nemesis.

Many reactions praised Fairy for raising the social issues. But nobody appeared to suggest some solutions. People tend only to blame the governments for failing to solve the burning social issues. But then a few geeks appeared as suggesting not to depend always on governments and leaders, but rather to work out solutions and to implement by civil societies at people's level...

∀ **salahkar**

- Guys! Almost tens of thousands of comments are there repeating the same opinion while praising Fairy, but nobody is talking about solutions. It's great that despite being a teenage child, she is highlighting the social issues and childishly asking God to take action. But it's a pity that mature elders either remain insensitive or behave like silent spectators.

Why are we always expecting everything from so-called leaders and authorities?

Why don't we, at public level, at civil society level should cohesively workout solutions and should implement at least at our level. Then let's see what happens.

Quickly, a pricking reaction fell down there from the troller....

∀ **Rose pricks**

- Not again. This guy, salahkar, seemed to be a motivational speaker. Bro! Millions of motivational speakers came and went and showered lots of wisdom. What's the use? Why is the world still sitting over all ages old problems? Why is India still struggling against all those chronic problems? Preaching alone can't resolve paining social issues, rather practicing rightly and timely can only serve the purpose of healing.

Better the preachers shell out their masks and come out from their comfort zones and should start implementing the self-proclaimed solutions in practical real-life.

The troll army jumped in to support their community.

∀ **risker**

• True, rose pricks is very much correct. Can any of these motor mouth preachers tell what they did in their lives to eradicate poverty in India?

The fact of the matter is that using their oratory skills, they are earning a lot, becoming richer day by day, by selling bubble dreams to naïve people. But doing nothing practically to improve the financial status of real poor people living in villages, small towns, or any corner of the nation.

I would like to ask these celebrity motivational speakers who often teach people how to get rid of poverty....What is their own annual income? How much tax do they pay, honestly? What percentage of their income or profits they donate to real poor people? You will never get honest answers.

If they are really concerned about the removal of poverty from India, then it is better they live for a few months or years amid real poor people, that also like them only with all round scarcity of food, money, and resources. Observe the nitty-gritty of poverty, retour social and socio-economic fabric of our nation, feel the pains, imbibe their psyche of desperations, expectations, and aspirations.

Mere donating money, food, clothes, and other things periodically are not going to help combat poverty. That may make them indolent and liable. Better attack the root cause of poverty by implementing better diversified work opportunities in current business forms or innovative forms.

∀ **ungyan**

- Not only job opportunities, but low-scale business models also with interest-free loan facilities. It may be on an individual, family, or community basis. In other words, establishing and enabling entrepreneurship for real poor people at grass root poverty line or below the poverty line.

∀ **lio**

- India is a nation of treasures of resources, talents, and lost traditional businesses. The need of the moment is strong willpower and a cohesive and inclusive approach by all factions of society.

"Garibi Hatao" is a slogan since independence blown by visionless political leaders, which remained mere slogan cyclically in every election, poor remained poor, been used as vote banks only.

So, don't expect anything from any government. They will use your pains as their gains.

Better civil societies come forward together and work out solutions like co-operative business organisations to make the poor stand on their own and gradually improve the quality of life.

∀ **shunya**

- Any damn solution won't be fruitful until and unless it ensures reducing the existing wide gaps in between haves and have-nots or simply in between poor and rich.

∀ **bhoomiputra**

- Flooding opportunities for poor people for better earnings won't help them in the true sense until & unless inflation can be brought under control. The fundamentals of economics clearly indicate that enhancement of per-capita income is useless if inflation keeps on rising beyond the affordabilities of people in society. So enabling earning more while carrying wider, deeper holes in pockets will not help anymore.

∀ **straight**

- But how will you make the poor earn more, in the absence of minimum basic education or training and at the same time also for the next-generation?

So don't jump the guns; educate them and train them before moving into new works or businesses.

I know that such trainings are already in practice in most of the existing businesses, but, seemed to be not adequate enough to get the so-called better results or better earnings compared to current scenario.

Meanwhile a mountain sized reaction popped up, which heated up the weather, because it was as parroty as it was in past...neither one can gulp nor can spew.

∀ **poetplanet**

- Shocked! I was surprised to see how digital warriors of the virtual troll army are marching directionlessly. An especially abled child, Fairy, is better than them, who harmoniously woven the lyrics in sync with the logical sequencing of issues; it would be better if they should learn and follow the same.

However, as usual, I don't want to waste time criticising anybody and will keep my comments sequentially. When will God revert to the mystery child? Nobody can guess. So, till then let's retour the issues and try to resolve at our level.

The first 4 verses are generic and filled with childish emotions. After a long leap, though, she appeared much grownup this time, maybe in her teenage. But, still a child, by voice, by body language through a well-sculpted body, by facial expressions through the gifted, well- chiselled face. Like in the past, she asked God a few questions and requested that they be solved.

The fifth verse, "Inflation," – is an everlasting unresolved phenomenon. Whatever political leaders and rulers say, all are hoaxes from the past, current times, and even will be in the future. Not only our nation but almost all the countries in the world are in the same boat. So, what's the way out? This domain is already flooded with could-be-pragmatic suggestions, and many more will be followed. Let's see who will prove practically right and who will deservingly earn the credentials?

The sixth verse, "Farmer's Suicide" also happened before and since after independence and even to date. Rulers came and went, always committed to resolving the unfortunate mystery, but not a single leader or government could fulfil the commitments. Reasons are quite evident, not only in our nation but all over the world. Misguided and divided farmers, especially small farmers, always fall victim to the unofficial corporatization of the farming sector and UNO's international farming treaties. The rich farmers are becoming richer; poor farmers are becoming poorer. Why? Because their requirement of financial needs often being fulfilled by dual loans rather than multiple loans. One loan is from the government; the second loan is from co-operative societies and, furthermore, loans from rich farmers or middlemen. Governments often waive off loans while farmers face losses in any adverse scenarios like natural calamities and insect attacks. Co-operative societies, too, treat softly. However, the loan providers from the communities of rich farmers and middlemen take such adverse situations, as an opportunity to ruin the poor farmers by taking over their small-scale farming property. Without hesitation, without any doubt, the last breed of loan providers are the real cause of farmers' suicide. I never behave politically correctly, so, guys, think it over and let's brainstorm how to help the poor living God of food on planet Earth.

The seventh verse, "malnutrition," is really sad that still a few population fractions of our nation are still deprived and sleeping at night without food when a larger population is celebrating the centenary period of independence. Still, food security is not in place, so we can utilise the left-out food for the needy. Still, we play with data only, insensitive to the harsh realities around us. Whenever any case is highlighted, everybody starts condemning the contemporary government, and governments start defending themselves by stating that previous governments are responsible for such a disastrous state of affairs. Many utilise such cases to shine their own public image. Let's start feeling shamefulness and do what is needed at our civil society levels.

The eighth verse, "poor rich gap" – it's a socio-economic disease since ages. It couldn't be healed.

History says that often, the poor became poorer, and the rich became richer. Because of policy paralysis in any form of rule, whether a kingdom or dictatorship or democracy by electoral politics, the poor's never been supported beyond the survival levels of livelihood & rich often been privileged beyond sky high limits. That's why the gap between rich and poor has always widened. Sorry, I don't have any idea how to make all the poor into rich. Do you have?

In the ninth verse, "Unemployment," – I heard from my great-grandfather that unemployment had been a problem since we got independence. Chronologically, there were many reasons for this social stigma. But, today mostly the, overpopulation is the main reason behind so-called unemployment. One more interesting point: generally, people misunderstand employment means as only the government jobs, whereas there are many suitable job opportunities always there available in the private sector for deserving candidates. So, it's not fair to beat hollow drums chanting "no jobs" or "no jobs," rather people should make themselves as deserving candidates for suitable jobs. They should even try for entrepreneurship in the fields of their core interests and natural forte.

The tenth verse, "corruption, terrorism, crimes," – History is a proven witness for all forms of crimes. The graph of crime fluctuated with the time. The then rulers tried their level best, but never ever succeeded in absolutely decriming their societies. A lot of scriptures have been written, a lot of wisdom has been spread, a lot of great men have taught great knowledge, and hardest and capital punishments have been practised.....but crime has never ever absolutely vanished from societies. Despite all those past negativities, let's not sit idle; let's do innovative brainstorming syncing today's modern age to work smart plans to decrime our societies to transfer a liveable place to our next-generation, which must be free from terrorism, corruption, all types of crimes......

As far as terrorism is concerned, if today's world is divided into 2 parts through the lenses of duly witnessed chronological credentials, it would be as pro-terrorist and anti-terrorist nations. Without any pseudoness and hypocrisy, the anti-terrorist nations must break all international ties and impose absolute sanctions over the nations who, in the past and still directly or indirectly advocate and practise terrorist & pro-terrorist practices.....

The eleventh verse, "rape and crimes against women," – is the most unfortunate filthy reality of human society since ages. Time and again women body have been the softest target for settling insane scores across civilisations; ultimately women bodies became battlefields, and even history witnessed a few pompous scriptures conceitedly encouraging followers for shaming womanhood. A lot of efforts have been made in the past and even in the modern age, but it seems as if everything went in vain. Surprisingly, in Sanatan and in a few more civilisations, women are worshipped like goddesses, but still, women are attacked as the softest link to demean potential rivals. So what exactly is required to eliminate the social curse – "rape" and "Crime against women?" Nobody has the right, honest answer. But, seeing this especially abled child's thought process, she is asking God to remodel men. This means redesigning the DNA of males, which can reform the prevailing psyche of males, who then never ever even can think of harming women by any means. When a child can think up to that extent, then why can't we matured do something rather to see what God can do?

The twelfth verse, "pollution and global warming," – with the rapidly growing global industrialisation period since last century, in the rat race for relatively much faster exponential growth, developed & then developing countries amassed pollution as an unavoidable byproduct. In turn, pollution gave birth to unanticipated evil global warming. Global warming already started showing its adverse effects, such as rising ambient temperature, erratic weather behavior, rapidly melting glaciers & rising sea levels, new airborne & waterborne diseases, and all these can't be said to be natural calamities but rather manmade disasters. These byproducts have never ever been envisaged by great scientists while self-boasting for so-called inventions of various science & technology wonders. Overall, it seemed as if humans of the modern age achieved growth at the cost of ungrowth. And even after sensing the horrendous results of pollution & global warming, global leaders are still playing hypocritically through pseudo-measures to curb the could-be disasters ahead out of pollution & global warming. But ultimately, who will suffer? The public only. So, when a child can think over these issues, why not at the civil society level we should start acting to improve the situation?

In the thirteenth verse, "rising population" – despite the majority of the population appears to agree with this issue and its aftermath, not only in India but the majority of countries across the globe, still the rapidly rising population is a major concern affecting the overall growth. Still, many societies and their people seemed inadvertently neglectful for various taboo reasons like lack of right education, lack of vigilant awareness, egoistic racism, unchallengeable religious doctrines in the name of God and a few more inexplicable toxic reasons. Whatever the reason, in this modern age, some or other way somehow everybody is suffering from the evils of overpopulation, and still, if we don't improve, then the coming generations will never ever forgive us. Scarcity of food, jobs, job opportunities, per-capita income, uncontrollable widening gaps in between have's & have-nots resulting in rising crime rates, and many more odds as byproducts of overpopulation are paining us. The time has come when every individual should feel a responsibility towards this social evil and must contribute by practicing population control measures so that a better, liveable place can be transferred to coming generations.

The fourteenth verse "intolerance" – It is sadly unfortunate that Bharatvarsh, India, timeless ageless Sanatan Dharma..... we Sanatanis, we Indians were known for our absolute divine doctrines of "Vasudhaiva Kutumbakam" (the whole world is a family), unity in diversity, respectfulness for co-existence, forgiveness, tolerance, and many more Earth-friendly, Cosmos friendly, Life friendly, Humanity friendly practices.....Whereas today we are called as intolerant. The fact of the matter is that despite invaders' cruelly bloodied suppressions a thousand years back, our holy values survived, but at the same time, they got contaminated, too. Now, in today's modern age, every now and then, the great moral value of tolerance is losing its glitter. Vote bank & appeasement-driven politics have distorted demographies and torn the social fabric, resulting in the loss of the essence of unity in diversity, creating unnecessary unpleasant power struggles at all levels of civil life and governance, in turn, grooming and escalating intolerance. It's really shameful! We Indians must come out of our hollow shallow silos of cast, color, creed, religion, must imbibe by Indianness as the only religion.....

The ideology of nation First could-be the only solution against the rising levels of intolerance.

The fifteenth verse, "wars" – Initially, long back when the human race was evolving from scratch to skies, wars were often fought for food, wealth, women, land, dominance, and survival. Later on in today's modern age, the human race has grown significantly well all-around, but wars are still happening every now and then. Again, the reasons are not very different, but they are selectively limited to land, resources, power, dominance, and struggle. After World War II, UNO and other international consortiums tried their level best as mere silent spectators to avoid the wars superficially, resulting in selectively justifiable wars supported by so-called superpowers and their allies. The unfortunate point is that when, after a lot of painful experiences, humans are mature enough to understand that wars can't be won by anybody, rather both sides lose the war by some or other means.....then why still often desperately jump into wars, ruining lives, and businesses of not theirs only, but almost globally. When global leaders often fail to ensure peaceful solutions, why not we, the common people, unite together globally and drive the movement for "NO WAR?" When protests often fail to stop WARS, let's innovate revolution using modern age technology. Finally, as usual, Fairy is requesting God for timely actions against all those social issues......when a child can think that way, why not we? Not only give it a thought..... but let's act!!!

Ancient golden words – one can't please everybody around. The same appeared this time again. Amid the continuous flow of responses, many positive reactions showered against that long comment by poetplanet. Again, a lot of blunt reverts gave poetplanet and its fans a bitter test. The troll army rushed fast, and most of them appeared to be reacting and focused on a single point of their preferred interest. A few comments from the troll army got highlighted with maximum no's of likes and dislikes parallaly.

∀ **whoru**

- I again request the app owner to block poetplanet. See, we don't need parroty. We don't need hollow preachers. We all know the problems in today's world. We need solutions. We need doers. Even if you can only speak, then learn to speak more in lesser words. What's the fun of ruining the valuable time of others with your nonsense?

∀ **scent**

- Very true. We are not directionless. Rather, the poetplanet has a faulty direction gauge. But it's our duty to show such people the right direction.

∀ **khatabahi**

- Right bro! Inflation is a long-lived disease in our system, but, in today's age of technology using AI and CI, we can get rid of this by further reforming the existing laws. I forgot the name, but remember that one popular learned man was advising on social media to abrogate all existing taxation laws and implement only one tax law. Restrict cash transactions maximum of up to 3 digits only using smaller denomination currency notes; for any transaction, make digital payments mandatory, and impose a 1% tax on each transaction. This will provide a transparent & corruption-less economy, generate more revenue for the government and, by saving loads of multiple taxes, will save money for people.

∀ **lone**

- Being from an agricultural background, feedback from the farmer community, I feel that a co-operative partnership system of farming for the community of small farmers can help to get rid of overly financial burdens.

∀ **grass**

- You are right. I have seen successful co-operative farming in a few parts of the country for different items like cotton, hybrid crops, sugar cane, honey, herbs, millet, flowers and a few more.

∀ **foody**

- It's really pathetic in today's age when, on the one hand, millions of poor people are still deprived of sufficient food, and on the other hand, many have more than sufficient food and don't even hesitate to waste it. The need of the moment is for the right implementation of laws like "Right For Food," "Food Security," and many more to ascertain food for everybody in today's world.

∀ **Richy rich**

- Guys! What's the nonsense!! The differences between the poor and the rich. It's not today's story. It has been in society since ages. No ideology as governance can minimise or fill the gaps in between rich and poor. The poor always dream of becoming rich, but the rich never ever imagine becoming poor. So the poor, who are at the receiving end, must learn the art of being rich from rich people and keep on working hard & smart with brains & brawns until they become rich through legal ways and means. When they succeed in becoming rich, then should starts supporting other people around them.

∀ **naukar**

- Friends! Unemployment, underemployment, and scarcity of jobs have existed since the independence of our nation. Various reasons were responsible for such unpleasant situations. But in today's age, it seems that overpopulation is the key factor. Apart from that misunderstanding for the word "Job," – many still think that "Job" means "government Job." "Private Sector Job" doesn't fit into their wish list. So, better we should improve ourselves in terms of population control and mindset for the nature of jobs to attain a workable balance between the quantum of job opportunities and the job-seeker population. More than that, if current and coming generations shift importance to vibrant entrepreneurship, then it may help by creating more jobs.

∀ **moral police**

- All types of crimes still exist despite a lot that has been done to control them, and a lot of solutions have been talked about. What's the way out? Can God help? I don't think so. Then what to do? Let's do inclusive brainstorming prudently………

∀ **neuro**

- What's this? Open-ended silence is also a crime. Don't always depend on Law & Order by Governments. There is no harm in making parallel armies like secret societies to counter the criminals in self- defense. Impose an absolute social boycott by the entire public around those who so ever identified as corrupt, criminal, terrorist, or sympathisers. Remember, any kind of criminal is a human, too, like us; counter them the way they dare to harm us…..Remember ancient golden words – Attack is the best defense.

∀ **nari**

- Nothing is more shameless than rape & any kind of crime against women. Have God helped at any time? Even God might not be remembering. Then what to do? How long generations after generations, gender bias to be tolerated? And why? Law & order, governments talk big, do less. No answers…….but then I was just perplexed by Fairy's words – Why don't you remodel men? This means remodeling male DNA….Hello scientists! Are you listening!! Can't you invent vaccines mandatory for male children, like other baby immunization vaccination courses…..to get moral & physical immunity against Satan's instincts of gender-biased male hood……may be the best use of technology for this and the next generations….

∀ co2

- Pollution and global warming are the most severe threats in today's world compared to any other. Remember the Covid period. How fresh and clear was the environment after the lockdown of many months? So, it's quite clear that we humans understand the language of threats better than any other. So, let's wedge war against pollution at the public level because, for long, governments have been acting just pseudo. Stop using all those things that generate directly or indirectly harmful pollutants and spread them into water, air, soil, noise, light, plastic, radioactive, thermal, visual, and gas pollution. Even EV vehicles driven by lithium batteries will be a threat to the environment in the next few years. The option of using hydrogen cars is also not feasible. We know it's not easy, but at least we can control or stop transportation using fossil fuel, air-conditioning, frozen food (cold storage), plastics, avoidable chemical & synthetic products, etc. It is better to legalise the use of ethanol-blended fossil fuels globally, where the percentage of ethanol should be as high as possible. More than that, proper recycling of plastic and electronic waste into alternative solutions. Once started, it may not be very difficult to get slower but steadier control over pollution and, in turn, over global warming.....else nobody will come down to rescue us from the sort of erratically increasing manmade natural calamities year on year like melting glaciers, rising sea levels, landslides, floods, cyclones, wildfires, rising scorching temperatures, severe snowfalls & frozen terrains, etc. So, let's start at our level.....

∀ world is family

- The serial population explosion is the mother of many problems in India and the whole world. The ratio of population vs resources, GDP, business & job opportunities, etc., is falling like welcoming to hell. Meanwhile, the ratio of population vs poverty, malnutrition, unemployment, intolerance, pollution, and crime are crossing limits. So, let's wake-up, let's get educated by alarm bells, and let's abandon mental blockades from scriptures and faiths. Because overpopulation was not a concern when scriptures were written, or faiths were created. Existing laws must be reformed with the provision of serious enforcement of population control rules & regulations against those who don't abide by them. Naysayers must be debarred from the Citizenship for rights and facilities.

∀ **cool**

- A lot is said about "tolerance" and "intolerance." But nobody came forward with a solution. And that's the biggest drawback of Democracy. So, what's the way out? When a child-like Fairy is compelled to ask God for help, what are we mature people waiting for? Using technology, let's link human-to-human connections nationwide all across the cast, color, creeds, and religions to build a tolerant society.

∀ **love & war**

- Wars have been happening since ages, and when will they stop happening, nobody knows. Still, a lot of direct or indirect wars are being fought in many parts of the world. UNO, religious leaders always failed. Can wars be avoided? Can the people of today's global society restrict their respective leaders from going into wars? In today's technology-enabled world, human societies across the globe can unite better than ever to compel their ruling leaders to avoid wars....by hook or crook. Even if dislodging them from power could be the right solution.

∀ poetplanet couldn't sit silent after many such responses from the troll army, fired back with much stronger words. The troll army intermittently followed back. Supporters of either side kept on jumping intermittently; this time, it seemed to be a little bit of an unhealthy environment....

As many people as many minds never ever help in concluding the odds.

The queer reel video posted by growing up teenager Fairy was telling her psyche, thought process, and emotional concerns for many social issues. Whereas social media nerds either venting out their hidden frustrations against everything coming across or playing the same music when somebody likes them.

Whatever, but this reel broke all the records of views, likes, and shares.....and there were smiles blinking on Fairy's face while intermittently watching the responses on her cell......

CHAPTER 5

Hi God! How are you?

Fifth Reel - Festival Of Democracy

03rd December

Fairy posted her 5th reel

Hi God! How are you?
I love my nation India, do you love too?
Elections time here, do you have in heavens too?
This time I also cast my vote, do you vote too?
Real issues being yelled, I told you before.
All parties promising tall, to win more.
Later real issues sidelined, religion became the only agenda.
Mother India was forgotten, Parties blowing religion propaganda.
'Abusing Democracy' becoming 'Democracy,' losing the directions.
'Pseudo Secularism' becoming 'Secularism' misleading the Nation.
All the Parties play hypocrite, tricking people by religions.
Rulers & opposition blaming each other, appeasing religions.
I wonder! In India there are no Indians in elections.
Indianness gone, casts & religions became vote banks.
History repeating again, Elections are only around Hindu or Muslim.
I am confused, are Indians means only Hindu or Muslim?

So, almost a couple of years later, after that long reel highlighting various issues of society, this new reel from Fairy brought odd sensations. By that time again, many had forgotten her as she was out of sight for a long time, but her diehard fans, who eagerly were waiting for her next reels, finally rejoiced. Many exhibited displeasure over her inconsistent presence on social media, but soulful fans didn't have any complaints.

Fairy started her social media journey long back when she was 4–5 years old, and to date, she has posted hardly 4-5 reels in due course of time spanning around 14-15 years.

Generally, the majority of people post and enjoy watching content that is full of a variety of blasting entertainment, such as informative knowledge, motivational, art, books, health, games, sports, religion, politics, community, etc. Unfortunately, various surveys indicate that adult, erotic & porn tops the chart in today's social media world, but decent forms of entertainment content, fairly sharable within families, are still trendy and giving tough competition.

Fairy's contents had neither an iota of glamourous sparkling entertainment value nor any formal information, but surprisingly, it not only broke existing records of viewership but also set new higher bars. That was also when she was not consistent enough in delivering content. A lot of analysis has been done throughout these years by social media experts, but never succeeded in concluding any convincing reasons behind her success.

As far as her fans are concerned, they had almost a common reason: the girl has stolen their hearts with her rarest divine innocence. They didn't have any complaints against her inconsistency, slurred voice, intoxicating eyes, dopey face, tottering wobbling steps, or nature of contents. The overall aura of her gracious presentations hypnotised the virtual audiences and made her a long-lasting cult.

This time, it also seemed to bring some unavoidable social issues prevailing in this great nation, but with a pinch of hot chilli & pepper.

As usual, netizens started throwing accolades and brickbats out of their psyche. The gauge of social media attributes was gearing up much faster with every passing time.

Out of millions of views and responses, few have been highlighted by ∀ co-netizens...

∀ **mango**

- Nice to see that Fairy has grown as a voter. Surprisingly, she is so sensible that at such an early stage, she understood the dark mysteries behind electoral politics in India. What she is saying is the naked truth......every time, elections are rigged by sidelining real issues and baking controversial Hindu-Muslim hatred as hotcakes. It's evident that fringe elements in politics and radical elements in religion often intend to divert Indians into their vote banks in the name of caste & religion. And all that has happened since independence by misusing democracy and secularism as proven shields.

∀ **proud Hindu**

- Mango! Don't talk hypothetically. Be specific. Talk with data and proofs. Who are the biggest democracy abusers? Who are real, and who are pseudo secular? If you have guts, speak out honestly, or else don't pollute the domain with half-cooked, open-ended junk.

∀ **Garv**

- Proud Hindu! Why are you asking? Why don't you enlighten people here?

∀ **Sara Jahan**

- Well said, bro! It's the easiest act to blame anybody. If one can question others, then one must be capable of listening and answering other's questions as well. I can openly say that all politicians, religious leaders, and Indians are responsible for the pathetic truth of every election in India.

∀ **nota**

- Again hypothetical. Case-by-case studies and analyses of elections since independence can clearly highlight that all such communal conflicts were engineered by political parties of certain specific ideologies that use the appeasement of minorities for the gains of vote banks. Blaming everybody is not logically correct.

∀ **near**

- Correct. I am bluntly saying that since independence, Muslim populations have been fooled by a few political parties out of their tested & proven ideology of appeasement of minorities. The cruel fact is that only a few Muslim leaders from politics, religion, business, and social work secretly benefitted in exchange for enriching the vote banks for those opportunistic political parties, but sadly, the rest of the entire Muslim population has been just only used and then been dumped inattentively till next elections.

∀ **Nazar**

- No, it's not fully true. If there is Muslim appeasement, then there is Hindu appeasement also. A lot of incidents are there in the public domain.

Meanwhile, another crowd-pulling message popped up outside of that boiling thread....

∀ **alert**

- It seems that Fairy is much more right than she appeared in this reel. See what she is saying – there are no Indians in India in the elections...but it seems true not only in real-life but also in virtual domains. It's not prudent to blame the likes of politicians, religious leaders, fringe elements, and radicals, but at the same time, we common men are also to be blamed. Why? We must realise that they are just a handful percentage of the entire population who often succeed in tricking & deceiving while influencing the common man. But we common men, despite awareness, still didn't learn the right lessons. In today's world of data, communication revolution, social media, AI, and CI, everything is much more transparent than before. So, why don't we utilise technology to unite the common man against the vested interests of those leaders who are still practicing appeasement as a tool to lure voters from minority sections of Indian society in the name of caste, religion, and status? Nothing is impossible in today's easily accessible & highly transparent world; we just need strong willpower, I mean to say stronger than those appeasers.

∀ **dtd**

- See, talking publicly and debating on social media or TV Channels are often fancy. However, implementing it practically is entirely difficult. The moment you start preaching to people against those powerful appeasement leaders, they will start either to eliminate you or force you to join them. They can't live without power or either as opposition. Appeasement is nothing but bribing selective sections of society to earn vote banks, and they have been doing it conveniently since many years without any vigilant resistance.

∀ **rare**

- So what's the way out? Should we start gathering like-minded people and start public awareness movements on roads or agitation in prime locations? Should we gather like-minded people to form a political party and fight against appeasing political parties? Or should we walk out of this country to get a job overseas and thus get rid of all the unsolvable social problems of poor India?

∀ **flier**

- Don't get carried away with half-backed thoughts & emotions. It's not always advisable to jump into the muck of electoral politics to clean it. Of late, history has witnessed how the then few aspiring activists turned politicians made a mockery of public expectations. Experimental activism or politics often ended up directionless, producing much worse leaders; the nation is already tolerating.

Meanwhile, the celebrity social media-savvy poet planet jumped in.

∀ **poet planet**

- Guys! What is going on? Everything is going directionless. Please stick to the content of Fairy, word by word. Verse 2 shows that Fairy has now grown-up well, rejoicing with happiness as she is eligible to cast her vote in the onset elections. At the same time, her childish side is also reflected when she asks whether elections are conducted in heaven, too. Whether God, too, cast a vote? Overall, it's quite clear that Fairy has grown-up physically but not mentally, which means she is still suffering from mysterious syndrome.

In verse 3, she kept on saying that during the election campaign, all the political parties, in their own ways, were trying to lure the public through fancy commitments against all the social & national issues. Fierce competition was building up among political parties to grab power.

Verse 4 shows the sudden transformation in the nature of political campaigns. As traditionally often happened in the past, while entering into the final phase of campaigning, the essential key issues of public interest were sidelined. "Mother India," "Mera Bharat Mahan," and "Unity in Diversity" were all holy slogans that were forgotten. The political rivalry narrowed down to showcase better well-wishers of selective religions.

In verse 5, time & again, the darker sides of democracy and secularism are highlighted. And that should be taken as an alarm bell. How does the misuse of constitutional ideology end up in questioning the sanctity of democracy and secularism? Still, we have time to improve; we should learn to avoid the misuse of democracy and biased secularism.

In verse 6, the innocent child, Fairy, noticed the darker side of electoral politics very rightly. By some or other means, all political parties are the same while fighting elections. One can refer to the historical archives and the differences between their commitments and achievements in report cards of their tenure. Always wide gaps clearly indicate the hypocritical side of their endeavours. The other shady side of political parties is their well-orchestrated appeasement of people from different religions. Since long back some parties have been practicing the appeasement of minorities, intending to earn an assured vote bank and, at the same time, blaming rival parties for appeasing majorities. The grey irony is that political parties are accustomed to running their political business mostly depending on appeasements only. Unfortunately, appeasement is not only in practice in the name of religion but in the name of caste, creed, demography, and language also. In today's modern age of the open world, people are well aware of the appeasement tricks of political parties but, somehow, always get trapped. No doubt, the common man is well aware, but awareness needs to be further intensified, and people should be enlightened to recognise the difference between appeasement and gratification.

In verse 7, what Fairy noticed is really pathetic. And that is not only in election times but always. There were viral stories and videos where a few foreigners were surprised when they didn't find a single person stating that I am Indian. Everybody they asked identified themselves either by their cast, creed, language, religion, or place. If you go to any foreign country, they will proudly introduce themselves by their country's identity. It's really shameful of us Indians; at least we should start training the next generations to proudly introduce themselves as – I am Indian, instead of by cast, creed, language, place, or religion.

Finally, in verse 8, the fairy opens Pandora's box of the harsh reality of Indian electoral politics. As happened historically, this time also, the election environment converged into the favorite agenda of politicians milking ever-green Hindu-Muslim conflict to earn as much as vote banks into their favor.

Honestly speaking, my position is also like Fairy's; all these issues have prevailed since the pre-independence era with erratic adverse effects on society and the nation as well, which damaged the expected growth cycles of India.

This time ∀ poetplanet's reaction was not taken sportingly and was marked as the weakest reaction ever by fans as well as troll army. Though fans shied away mostly from reacting, but, the troll army seemed not willing to spare and was bombarded with the harshest reactions.

∀ Jago India Jago

- I am feeling offended not only with ∀poetplanet but with everybody for the passive responses against a child's eye-opening concerns, which are crying out for rightly and timely action to make our nation nuisance-free from prevailing vices ruining India.

Fairy's expressions are out of real observations, asking for real concrete solutions, even if she is requesting God to do so. But people like poetplanet, out of their mental bankruptcy, kept on presenting themselves as parroty, interested in self-styled shallow preachings only along with hollow solutions.

Enough is enough! I am going to file public litigation cases against concerned politicians for the lacuna in commitment vs achievement in the last tenure and violation of the law by using religious discrimination. Are there any lawyers in this thread who can take my case?

∀ light in tunnel

- Kudos! Can't explain in words. What a direct & bold step. Jago! India needs people like you. I am with you. I am a retired lawyer from the Supreme Court. I will speak to my lawyer community, who could join us voluntarily. Will DM once get through?

∀ **Jago**

- Thanks, sir, for your prompt response. Let's start! Mere talking and debating won't do. Please try to add as many as possible to make a strong team to fight against the crooked political shenanigans.

So, the essence of this communication changed the ambience of running threads. Few netizens responded posing as lawyers and then started connecting through DM's.

Surprisingly, for the first time ever, few comments pulled attention to the style of writing & use of words. It seemed as if they were posted by school & college-going children of different age groups.

∀ **I'm a kid**

- Hi Uncles & Aunties! I watched Fairy's reels and liked them all. She always appeared to be suffering from some mysterious disease, but still, she raised social issues better than mature people. That's really great. But, this time, when she raised the issue of Hindu-Muslim, that's really disturbing. Why do all roads of elections lead to Hindu-Muslim always? It's really bad for India.

∀ **India**

- Hello Uncles! I feel that we should learn from Fairy, especially all people from the age of my mom & dad. When a child-like Fairy can speak without any fear, exposing the wrong things going on in India, then it is the duty of all seniors to look into that and resolve the bad issues.

∀ **doll**

- Yes! My dad told me that elections come once in 5 years. I remember that generally, there is peace in our city, but whenever elections come, a lot of brawls, fights, killings, and curfews happen. I don't know why? TV News channels always show debates full of hatred and news of fighting Hindu-Muslim. Even newspapers are full of such bad news. Generally, my mom & dad never allow us to watch the news or read. But, after watching Fairy's reel, when I asked my mom & dad, I just went mad at what they told me about the Hindu-Muslim fights since from many years in past.

∀ **chunchun**

- I am also feeling very bad after watching Fairy's this reel. In her old reels, she sang about the problems of being an especially abled child, health & education for children, and many painful issues of our country. But this reel about elections and the Hindu-Muslim angle is very disturbing. Ours is an international school where children of India from Hindu, Muslim, Christian, Sikh, and many other religions, as well as a few children from foreign countries, study in a peaceful continental environment. We never saw any bit of a fight between Hindu and Muslim children. But, after this reel, I am afraid to visualise that after some years as a grown-up adult, I will have to be part of such a society where there are religion-based fights. Then, I don't want to grow up and don't want to live in a society where Hindus and Muslims often fight.

∀ **Satya**

- I am disturbed. I am Hindu, and I have many Muslim friends. Right now, we are in the 10th standard. We never felt like hating or fighting each other. Though sometimes in TV News and newspapers, we saw news of clashes between Hindus and Muslims that never affected our friendship. Our Muslim friends always participated with us in celebrating our Hindu festivals, such as Raksha Bandhan, Ganpati, Durga Pooja, Deepawali, Holi, etc. And they always invite us to their festivals of Id. But this reel shook us badly.

∀ **little master**

- Why do these leader uncles divide people in Hindu-Muslim? We children in school never feel like that. But after watching Fairy's reel, I also fear that we children, after growing up when going to vote, will fight as Hindu-Muslim.

∀ **mama pride**

- Fairy used complicated words like – 'abusing democracy,' 'pseudo secularism,' 'appeasement,' 'Indianness.' I am annoyed to know why our previous generations of mom & dad are still bearing these bad things. Why are they not solving all these issues? Do they want us also to live with all this muck? We generally watch entertainment and sports stuff on social media and TV or play mobile games. Hardly watch any sensible stuff like this reel about issues that seriously disturbing society. Thanks to Fairy, whose songs alarm a wake-up call about the dirty faces of our society and indirectly ask for quick-fix solutions.

∀ **big boy**

- After watching all this dark stuff, my heart is saying that I will not vote when I grow to that age. Why should I become a puppet in the hands of political uncles, and why should I offer myself to appease me? My father is a self-made man. He often says that you never ever depend on anybody; you believe in yourself and depend on yourself only. He always says that he is a proud Indian. Whatever he wanted in his life, he earned on his own with hard work and honesty. He hates politics and politicians and has never voted. So, I will do that.

∀ **dancing doll**

- We did everything together in school, but we never felt any differences among us. But Fairy's song shows pictures that are just the opposite. When I asked my Muslim friends in school, they responded with similar feelings to me and other Hindu students. But after growing up, if we will have to live with the same boiling hatred as the current situation in election times, then better I would like to leave this place and will go where there are no Hindu-Muslim fights.

∀ **cold**

- I also feel the same like dancing doll. But when I asked my mom, she told me that if I went to any place in our country, everywhere, I had to face this. You better live in areas where the majority of people from your religion live, or else you will have to face the heat of hatred, whether it's a Muslim or a Hindu. Politicians use both Hindus & Muslims as vote banks in election times, and then, after winning or losing, ignore them till the next elections. All this is not happening only in current times but has been happening for centuries. Though our forefathers and previous generations couldn't solve the Hindu-Muslim mystery, we children from this generation must take it as a challenge and must solve it at any cost.

∀ **flier**

- We children must unite and write a letter to the President of India to take action against these political uncles who are doing all these bad things to Hindus and Muslims and to our great nation, India.

∀ **eyes**

- What president can do? Nothing. Check the chapter on political science in the subject of social science. It clearly shows that the Indian president doesn't have the power to take direct action against any miscreants. So, it is better we children at our level start thinking about solving this nonsense of Hindu-Muslim fighting so that a few years from now, when we grow up, we will have a peaceful society in which to live. Our father's generation and forefathers wasted their time getting fooled by politicians, fighting, and demeaning each other, but we shouldn't waste it!

∀ **watch**

- Why is everybody shouting Hindu-Muslim? Fairy has not said anything about Hindu-Muslim fights. She is saying that in elections, politicians are trapping Hindus and Muslims as vote banks by tricking them with false commitments. At the same time, people are using democracy freehandedly as freedom of expression for doing wrong things only. Similarly, true secularism exists in Law Books only; in real-life, politicians are using it as pseudo secularism. Fairy is saying that in elections, the real necessary issues are being forgotten by politicians, and finally, they start competing with each other only in the name of religion. Overall, there are no words in her song as Hindu-Muslim fights. Unnecessarily, we school children are doing the same thing as many social media-savvy by blowing hatred.

Many more comments continued by people from all walks of life and all age groups, including students from schools and colleges. After the comment of the watch, people started realising that nowhere Fairy is telling that Hindus and Muslims are fighting with each other. But rumour mongers were not learning any lessons and still continued polluting the ambience of the public domain.

Within minutes, one teacher jumped in and cautioned students to stay away from such social media rumours. Few more experts from the different fields follow suit.

∀ **Principal Bharat school**

- Hello, children! Whichever school you are from, please stay away from social media propaganda of any type of political or elderly content. Like all of you, I am also a fan of Fairy. But it doesn't mean that I shouldn't check the contents of her reel microscopically. Even the comments and reviews from many fans are also to be evaluated before reacting, if time permits you, from your routine life, studies, and necessary work. I was going through a few comments from others and then from children as it appeared, and I was surprised at how people blindly follow the half-cooked rumours. Thanks to ∀ the Watch, who highlighted the correct version of Fairy's song and identified the mistakes of fellow netizens, there was no mention of Hindu-Muslim fights.

I request the parents to handle the situation carefully and enlighten their children for truthful behavior. At the same time, I would like to request that the app management to look into the matter with a serious note and debar those who post falsified messages. Finally, I would like to request police & Cyber Cells have close watch over social media polluters.

∀ **neuro**

- Hi, I am a psychologist, and I watch Fairy Reels often. I'm a fan of her, too. But this time, the nature of the content has been a little bit volatile. It's not exactly inflammatory but slightly tangent. Many of us know a famous old saying - politics is the last refuge of scoundrels. Time and again, it has been proven by some or other deeds of politicians. There is no doubt that, in a democracy, people have the ultimate power to elect a leader, but, of late, democracy has become the pivotal pain point in the system. Abusing, overusing, and pseudousing of democracy has become the new normal of democracy. The sobbing democracy has been further wounded by pseudo secularism. Political aspirations are so blind that power-hungry political parties and their leaders are out to do anything, whether it is legal or illegal, moral or immoral, just to grab the power. We, common people, must understand politicians' behavior and shouldn't get carried away by their self-proclaimed doctrines.

∀ **hormone**

- Hi! I am a behavioral science expert. Let me put the whole ongoing controversy in easy language. Is Fairy's reel is obscene? No. Is the fairy's reel dirty? No. Is Fairy's reel offensive? No. Is Fairy's reel is derogatory? No. How can Fairy's reel be labelled as controversial? I am surprised. See a teenager, especially an abled child, who just attained the age of a legalised voter, expressing her observations during the election period in a rhymer way. Her rhymes have neither fire nor smoke. So, why are we all shouting hue and cry for her true soulful expressions out of her rare childish innocence?

As usual, a lot of wisdom and leg-pulling continued for a long, again breaking previous records of viewership, comments, and likes.

The common thing in all responses was that despite the so-called controversial nature of that reel, people remained loyal fans of Fairy. Netizens were either supporting some or trolling others, and the threads continued beyond wild imaginations.

CHAPTER 6

Hi God! How are you?

Sixth Reel - Who is the Greatest God?

03rd December

Fairy posted her next reel.

Hi God! How are you?

Hatred all-time high, are you worried too?

Communal violence in elections, mocking Law & Order,

Leaders safe in AC heavens, innocents suffered torture.

Shady men fearlessly looting, burning properties and pelting stones,

Police helpless as usual, finding safe zones.

Bodies kept falling, but, voting kept rolling,

Votes costlier than lives, rotten face of polling.

Muslims say only their God is great, Hindus say their Gods are timelessly great.

I am confused, upset, please come down and decide whose God is great?

'God created human' said old wise, 'human created God' said new wise.

I am again confused, please clarify who created whom when and why?

History says, Holy Greater India and Sanatan Dharm are since millions years.

Invasions shortened it into today's India and Sanatan as Hindu since thousand years.

Hindus blame Muslims for their shady aspiration for Ghazwa-e-Hind,

Muslims blame Hindus for their natural aspiration for Hindu Rashtra.
Leaders cunningly deluding both, only for grabbing power,
Their haunting aspirations, wounding India and damaging future.
Then I wonder why you are so insensitive, inactive & only watching silently always?
Are you like those autocrat leaders, and interested only as being God anyways?
Come here & tell Indians what is the supreme significant? Religion or Nation?
Nationalism must be the only religion to give better future for coming generations!
I am invoking you, come down to solve religion's filthy malfunctions.
Solve the cursed Hindu-Muslim conflict, save India from scary extinction.
Hi God! Reverse the TIME, make it Holy Greater India again like pre-invasion.
Quickly soon re-reverse the TIME, to make India peaceful Super Power again.
Leaders are always wasting time, by fracturing public decisions.
I hope You only can do! You don't need anybody's permission.

Even though earlier known as an inconsistent social media celebrity, Fairy, the global sensation, shocked her fans by posting the next reel within a few hours after the previous controversial reel in late evening on the same day. And this time, Fairy created provocative sensations across the globe with bluntly naked, truthful verses.

Though it was election time, the socio-political environment was full of insane inhuman examples in many places and angst against the system from common men and the so-called human rights activists was also at an all-time high.

The election commission, central government and state governments were struggling and trying their level best to control the law-and-order situation.

But fans couldn't resist their emotions, and the public domain was flooded with a tsunami of responses. Though the internet was banned in many places, but, App ∀ users were unaffected. Thanks to the next-generation AI & CI.

As usual, within a few minutes after the reel was posted, responses started pouring in one by one, then speed kept on escalating continuously, and then, like a cloud burst, high cusec floods. The AI & CI spontaneously mark the rating of responses, which enables users to read the selective stuff based on merits.

So, a few responses with the best ratings pulled the attention of netizens and comments, likes as well, and integrated into endless threads.

∀ holy

- Prima fascia: this reel is the mother of all the reels from Fairy. In a nutshell, it shows a naked mirror to our hibernating society. Whatever you do in your life, whatever status of your existence, your life in its entirety gets shacked during elections. Because since thousand years ago, while invasions started, and the pre-independence communal incompetence of India was being inherited by the political system after the independence till date, nurtured and selectively been used directly or pseudo by power-hungry political leaders.

All the high-priority real issues get overshadowed by communal appeasement because of its darker glittery ability to earn vote banks. Should we wait for God to come down to clear the clutter of religious phobia? Should we wait for the birth of a great Hero or demigod to convert religious rivalry into nationalism? Thousand years passed after invasions, approx. century passed after independence; how many centuries will it take to enable

India to reinstate its glorious heritage of millions of years of holiness? Don't know!

∀ **Indy**

- In today's world, everybody knows about anything and everything. So, there is no need to try to repeat the same facts and figures again and again. Better to explore permanent subjective as well as objective solutions.

See, miscreants are always milking opportunities during elections or any other occasions. I mean to say the influencers and actors are orchestrating Hindu-Muslim rights every now and then. Surprisingly, there are a handful of fringe elements, hardly approx. 10% on either side means Hindus and as well as in Muslims, who threaten & spoil the life of the majority of the population, approx. 90%. It's a tragic reality that the 90% neutral population always fails to control the said 10% fringe elements, and innocents are left helpless to be butchered and looted.

Politicians always play blame games, even though everybody understands and knows that only autocratic political ambitions and deceitfully layered corroded ideology of politicians responsible for communal rights have happened so far. Politicians are highly skilled in silently secretly creating Hindu-Muslim rights, then playing blame games, then assuring and showing off as controlling the situation, and then claiming credits for damage control. Thus, mastering the art of manipulating the Hindu-Muslim conflict tool to earn credentials and vote banks at the cost of character assassination of rivals and assassinating innocent citizens, social fabric, and growth of the nation.

The government & system always work in reactive mode, though it is always proactively claimed that the law & order situation is intact.

Ultimately, who suffers? We common people only. Few miscreants only get convicted, and many get free unscratched. The political leaders and system operators claim the job done and justice done in the course. Public memory is very short. Despite all the unrepairable wounds, this cycle get repeated next time while in similar situations.

The question arises: when will it end? When in India Hindu-Muslim conflict will end? When will Indians learn the lesson? Oh……my God! I just forgot!! Even Fairy also sang in her previous reel — there are no Indians in India!!! I have given up……I am lost…..

∀ **rise**

• Not only politicians but social and religious leaders also played decisive roles in such rights.

Remember those viral videos in the public domain, where religious leaders are blowing inflammatory speeches to provoke their followers to take the law into their own hands to teach lessons to the opponents? This means Hindu religious leaders provoke Hindus against Muslims. And Muslim maulanas and religious leaders provoke Muslims against Hindus. This has been happening since pre-independence.

So, leaders from politics, social work, and religion all tried their level best to retain their power intact at the cost of the loss of lives of innocents.

And what resulted out of an unpleasant communal grudge? Unfortunately, this holy land was divided into 3 nations.

India patiently continued inheriting its rich cultural and moral heritage, managed so well by all means, and became one of the top 3 global superpowers.

Whereas another unfortunate piece, made out of religious animosity, named as Pakistan, is on the verge of collapse. Credit goes to its shady leadership, which chronologically misguided & blinded the people by manipulating the incepted ideology of a religion-based country and as the only supreme important glory of their life and parallaly hollowed their nation by practicing corruption as their birthright. The all-round comparison with India has opened the eyes of people in the religion-based rouge nation Pakistan, and now they have started realising that the division of India into 2 nations was an irreparable mistake.

Formation of any country based on religious animosity or religious supremacy couldn't help people; rather, such a phenomenon will ruin their lives forever. The same thing people of today's India must understand, particularly the Muslims, who are dreaming of Ghazwa-e-Hind. Because the religious leaders using the ideology of religious animosity & supremacy are always interested in their own vested interests, and they always misguide the gullible people in the name of religion to fulfil their own vested aspirations. Once the power is achieved, then that insanely grabbed power brings thick corruption, as it happened in Pakistan.

∀ **light in tunnel**

- It's really pathetic when we see visuals of violence & brutal killings around voting centres and voting going on parallaly, while police are watching helplessly. Sometimes, somewhere, it seems as if it is state-sponsored from behind the scenes. If the government can't control such violations of law-and-order, then it shouldn't conduct elections as such to blacklisted election centres. If the government don't take any action, then people should boycott voting. I and my family suffered a lot from such consequences, and that's why I am highlighting this issue.

∀ **Sufi**

- After suffering massive losses of life & property while thousands of Hindu-Muslim rights for centuries, why still, in today's modern age, people of both sides get carried away by hatred provocations? Hindu-Muslim rights are a curse on Bharat, brutally experimented on by invaders to divide the people of this great nation. Now, there are no invaders, so why to allow animosity rights? Better everybody should focus on the inclusive growth of India to regain its lost status of super power by all means.

∀ **eventer**

- I am running a global event management company. I have many Muslim friends in India as well as from many foreign countries who are well-educated and doing very well either in jobs or business. Many times, I discussed with them about this peculiarly weird issue of Ghazwa-e-Hind. You will be surprised that 90% of Muslims don't support this scripture's orthodox radical concept. Hardly 10% of Muslims are comprised of radicals as political leaders, religious leaders, their blind followers, and illegal migrants as appeased vote banks…… They are carrying forward the dreams of Ghazwa-e-Hind, supported by a few international Muslim terrorist groups.

The 90% of Muslims understand and believe that for peaceful life in today's global society, the basic principles of humanity to be imbibed like "Live & Let Live," "co-existence of different ideologies or faiths, cast, color, creed," "humanity is the ultimate religion," nationalism is the only religion."But, one twist is there, most of them fear to say it openly, guessing harassment from radicals. At the same time few Muslim friends are very courageous, can say truth bluntly in public domain. So, this insane slogan of Ghazwa-e-Hind will soon die its own death like Pakistan, because it is born out of "Religious Fanaticism" and its byproduct "Hatred," and hatred doesn't last long.

Now let's see the other side, "Hindu Rashtra" aspired by Hindus. If we can conduct a global public opinion poll, you will be surprised to know that the majority of people respond by saying that it's already Hindu Rashtra, why unnecessarily confuse? After the division of the then undivided India in 1947, when Pakistan was made as an Islamic Nation, then automatically, the rest of India, having Hindus as the majority, became a Hindu Nation, even though people from other religions were allowed to co-exist respectfully.

You go anywhere in the world, once you tell that you are from India, the first response with good regards will be, "Oh Hindu" or "Oh Hindi".......

Even my Muslim friends shared their experiences in any foreign country, whenever they introduce themselves with their name and as from India, 99% of the time, the first response they get is, "Oh, Hindu-Muslim" or "Oh, Hindi-Muslim."

So, that's the power of the glorious image of great Bharat, Bharat as Hindu Rashtra, even though unworded in books of the Constitution of today's age.

If you can remember, how Indians stuck in any foreign country in force majeure or war situations were respectfully allowed safe passage to return to India. Remember the beginning of the Ukraine War. Even almost all the stuck-up Pakistanis also presented themselves as from India by carrying Indian flags in their hands. So, the concept of Hindu Rashtra is immortal even if not made official.

∀ **missing God**

In any part of the world, God is the cause of all sufferings of human beings. Fairy asked the right question: who created whom, when and why? God-fearing people wouldn't like the stuff where God is questioned. Some will hear and forget without responding. Some will say it's blasphemy and wage religious war against it. Whatever your faith is, your God will never ever come to rescue you from troubles. It's an endless debate....

The truth is that those who don't depend on God for any need are much better humans than those who blindly believe in their God and, at the same time, blindly hate other's God.

So, what to do for a better peaceful life? For a better, peaceful world?

Don't complicate it; make it simple. Conduct yourself with unworded or worded ideology, according to what basic principles of humanity say, and, for any damn thing, don't waste your time in waiting for God till God can afford to come...

∀ right or wrong

- One can understand that being an especially abled child Fairy can speak out about any illogical stuff which could not be righteous enough. But well-educated, well-doing people are behaving like Penny Wise Pound Foolish.

Everybody knows that "Divide and Rule" is an old political formula initiated by Britishers while invading India and widely actioned till dividing into 2 Nations. And then post-independence, the same formula was recycled by inheritors, who were Indian by the body and Britisher by the mind.

The majority of people in this country understand all these cruel facts, but sleeping with a fully loaded belly, because either they never got hurt directly by well-orchestrated communal violence or safely hiding in their inaccessible silos.

People who suffer can only imitate the pain of losing near & dear ones and losing property.

Governments and systems exist, but there are no foolproof preventive measures. They often act either in fire-fighting or in reactive mode only, and often fail in damage control and damage recovery.

∀ proud Muslim

- If one sees all the comments, the majority of people somehow favor Hindus only and have fixed biased opinions over Muslims as well-known islamophobia. Every time when some communal incidents happen, all the machinery comes out to vilify Muslims only. Why? Aren't the Hindus arrested recently responsible for communal violence? Why only Muslims are arrested being said to be responsible?

Nobody responded to ∀ proud Muslim, while all the ongoing threads continued separately.

After some time, one more Muslim guy entered, responses from both communities started sparkling in, and eventually, a simmering thread went on pulling.....

∀ **Rabkidua**

First of all, why are such posts allowed on social media, which provokes hatred among Hindus and Muslims? And why specifically are Muslims targeted only always?

∀ **poet planet (jumped in)**

Please don't shoot in the dark. Check the facts. A few days back, when she posted the reel "Election the celebration of Democracy," voting was already over few days back. She might have witnessed or watched the incidences on TV News channels, social media platforms of hatred speeches by leaders of all political parties & religion groups, communal violences by miscreants.

When this fresh reel was posted after a few days, by that time, elections were over, and many incidents of communal violence had been reported. Meanwhile, the Police came into action and arrested many miscreants from both communities in many places in India.

So, where the provocative elements are in her rhymes which influenced people for communal rights? She posted this reel after all the miscreants had been arrested, thanks to CCTV cameras, drone cameras, AI, and CI.

Again lessons learned is that rather than reactive measures with the help of science & technology, we must work out for innovative tools for preventive measures against such rights.

Fairy is innocent.

∀ I love Islam

Totally disagree with poet planet. What does it mean that Fairy posted reels after the incidents? Still, her reels might add fuel to the fire. Whatever she sang in her reel is against Islam. A true Muslim can never forgive her.

∀ Village maulana

- Totally right. Fairy is seen abusing Islam and Allah. She has committed blasphemy.

∀ Bhai Chara

- ∀ I love Islam and ∀ village maulana; how can you say that Fairy has abused your religion or committed blasphemy? Nowhere had she uttered the word "Islam" or "Allah." Then, unnecessarily, don't drag the innocent child into communal controversy.

∀ Bademiyan

- Though she has not spoken anything abusive directly, but What is the meaning of saying that *"Muslims say only their God is great?"* It's a truth that Allah is the only God and supreme. If somebody is denying or challenging, then it's blasphemy.

∀ Bhaichara

But in the same phrase, she is singing that *"Hindus say their Gods are timelessly great"* and then *"I am confused, upset, please come down and decide whose God is great?"* So, it clearly shows the innocence of a child. In a democracy, everybody has the right to express their opinions or to ask any question. And democracy is the right given by the constitution. This Nation is governed by the constitution. So, if an especially abled child, out of curiosity, is asking God to clarify which God is better, then what's the harm in it?

∀ I love Islam

- Don't play with words. Fairy has done wrong, and she has to pay the price.

∀ **I love Hindu**

- What will you do? Don't pollute the ambience of this virtual world. Why are you behaving like fanatics creating a ruckus?

∀ **Proud Hindu**

- Never ever dare to touch Fairy.

∀ **Proud Muslim**

- Anybody committing insolence in the glory of Allah has to face the dire consequences.

∀ **Ghazwae Hind**

- XxxxxxxxxTRUNCATEDxxxxxxxxxxx

∀ **Muslim Brotherhood**

- XxxxxxxxxTRUNCATEDxxxxxxxxxxx

∀ **All India Muslim**

- XxxxxxxxxTRUNCATEDxxxxxxxxxxx

∀ **Muslim unity**

- XxxxxxxxxTRUNCATEDxxxxxxxxxxx

∀ **Great Hindu**

- XxxxxxxxxTRUNCATEDxxxxxxxxxxx

∀ **Jai ho**

- XxxxxxxxxTRUNCATEDxxxxxxxxxxx

∀ **Pawan**

- XxxxxxxxxTRUNCATEDxxxxxxxxxxx

∀ **Akhand Bharat**

- XxxxxxxxxTRUNCATEDxxxxxxxxxxx

∀ **Ganga Jamuna**

- XxxxxxxxxTRUNCATEDxxxxxxxxxxx

∀ **Deedaremaula**

- XxxxxxxxxTRUNCATEDxxxxxxxxxxx

∀ **Only Islam**

- XxxxxxxxxTRUNCATEDxxxxxxxxxxx

∀ **Proud Rohingya**

- XxxxxxxxxTRUNCATEDxxxxxxxxxxx

∀ **Jehad**

- XxxxxxxxxTRUNCATEDxxxxxxxxxxx

∀ **srtansejuda**

- XxxxxxxxxTRUNCATEDxxxxxxxxxxx

Hundreds of thousands of responses have been fully truncated by this cult app ALL "∀," thanks to its next-generation AI & CI.

That was the beauty of ALL…It never ever allows content carrying the essence of any obscene, derogatory, offensive, abusive, hatred, fanaticism, or inhuman stuff.

When virtual miscreants realised that their responses were being absolutely truncated under their IDs, it somehow annoyed them with the feeling of being demeaned publicly, but they seemed as if not ready to learn lessons. And most of them again posted almost similar stuff. ALL truncated those nuisances again. And then suddenly, an advisory is received by all its users who were in some, or other way connected with Fairy's recent reel…

Advisory To ALL ∀ Users

Please consider this communication as a final warning to those who will be found to have failed to abide by the Terms & Conditions of ALL ∀.

Such users will be blocked forever and may be subjected to legal action.

So, such was the SOP of ALL for its users. And that's what made it the No. 1 App consistently for many years.

People must have understood that if ALL wanted, they could haven't even published the truncated versions. But their management wanted to convey a strong, loud, and clear message that insane illicit nuisances shouldn't be posted on this social media app; they aren't going to entertain any radicals, maniacs, sadists, lunatics, hypocrites, hollow, spineless, inhuman from any cast, faith, religion. ALL was not like other apps, which keep silent or promote anti-social or inhuman filth.

One can understand the dire seriousness of ALL ∀'s advisory. Though those truncated response were not seen by anybody, all those were confined to the archiving of the app.

If a hacker could-be able to hack ALL ∀'s servers, the world might witness those guttery, filthy responses ornamented with unparliamentary speeches and melodious abuses targeting mothers & sisters.

Where Muslims were expressing that Fairy's rhymes and Hindu netizens' comments hurt their religion & God and threw the worst possible hatred-filled allegations against Fairy and Hindus. In retaliation, Hindus were responding to Muslims with the worst possible blame, highlighting that Islam was the most intolerant religion, which doesn't respect any other religion in this human world.

The offline social life, TV News, TV debate shows, print media, social media channels…..as usual, all were passively breathing silently amid the uncomfortable pollution of Hindu-Muslim communal unrest, but it was ALL ∀ which proactively took necessary action against all those state or non-state actors and players from both the communities without any prejudices.

Similar actions could have been expected from learned representatives from both communities who have good heads over their shoulders and guileless hearts, ...even though governments will act reactively, and the law will take its own course, somewhere, this communal pandemic must be stopped...........

Meanwhile, Fairy's fame crossed the invisible boundaries of virtual worlds and entered into the reality world of live TV Debates. This time, her reel again crossed the earlier records of viewership and, at the same time, appeared as indirectly influencing people's lives out of so-called sensitively religious content. TV news channels, as usual, rushed in a rat race to milk such opportunities to earn TRP as much as possible. A social media app can ban objectionable content, but a pinch of such obnoxious content is essential for live debate shows.....Thanks to the fourth pillar of democracy, "Media" - TV-media houses, the sponsors of debate-participants who believe that TV Debates have great potential in shaping their credentials and last but not least, the TV-media friendly laws. Unfortunately, the majority of TV viewers enjoy such street dog fights on debate shows.

BTW while all those nuisances, poet planet's detailed demonstrative post was also published along with many more virtuous responses from decent people, but unfortunately, there were no takers because all were poking their heads to have a look at the filthy stuff being served with high-energy levels, though those were negative energies......

As the words of legal action reflected in ALL's advisory, many responses started focusing on legal actions.

∀ **Jago India jago**

- So, now people can understand that in response to the previous reel of Fairy, why I emphasised legal action against those miscreants responsible for disturbing peace & harmony by spreading inter-religious hatred.

Discussions, arguments, and debates in text form or in ALL-Live form or in ALL-podcast form wouldn't solve the perennial issue of communal hatred and communal violence.

It can either be solved by a change of heart through counselling & education or by absolute enforcement of law-and-order. If reforms are required to plug the loop holes of existing law, then it should be done with immediate effect. Because historically there are lot of observations, where the lawyers of miscreants manipulated the loop holes and succeeded in setting free their repetitively tainted clients.

Now, I have decided and am going to lodge a PIL against all those politicians and religious leaders whose viral hatred speeches are in the public domain, which provoke public sentiments from both communities.

∀ Indian maulana

- I am going to lodge a case on Fairy for blasphemy.

Many users with IDs resembling Muslim names or words followed the outrage against Fairy, but without violating decency this time. Few of them got responses as advice for introspection.

Few users with Hindu names or words as their IDs also posted messages declaring legal action against Fairy. But most of them have been trolled for acting as pseudo secular.

Similarly, many users with Hindu names or posing as Hindus also posted similar messages highlighting legal action against so-called pseudo seculars from political and religious breeds from different ideologies.

Few daredevils declared taking legal action against the app management ALL ∀. Surprisingly, ALL didn't truncate their posts.

Tensions kept on building across every nuke and corner of the country....

Fairy's effigies have been burnt at many places.......

ALL's effigies have also been burnt in many places.....

Minutes ticking fast into hours, hours ticking fast into days.......

Just a couple of days passed, and Fairy got the very first legal notice at her doorstep.....Before she and her family could recover from the shock, one by one, many legal notices started knocking at her doorstep.....

Thanks to sincere co-operation from ALL ∀ management and Cyber police, the FIR's registered at Indra Prasth police Head Quarter been delivered at Fairy's postal address, which was mysteriously unknown till date.

Such FIRs from many parts of the country continued to drop at her doorstep.

Being especially abled, Fairy was quite unaware of the seriousness of FIR's. But her parents were feeling it very difficult to absorb terrible shocks from such legal actions. Somehow, her parents managed to get a renowned lawyer to handle those cases.

There is one infamous saying since the independence of this country –

"Do whatever you can do, talk whatever you can talk, but finally, all the roads lead to Hindu-Muslim nuisances only."

Unfortunately, that exactly happened with Fairy, as well, with mountains being made out of molehills.

Real-life observations truly rhymed into reels and without any vested interest shared in the virtual world, liked by many, hated by many......but, coincidentally, because of instilling pinch of communal flavour in her song, finally she was destined to face the heat of Hindu-Muslim joint venture of white collared pseudo-seculars and fanatic homo-sapiens.

CHAPTER 7

Hi God! How are you?

Unjustice

A few days after 03rd December

Supreme Court

Indra Prasth Nagar

Capital of Bharat

The Supreme Court campus was hugely crowded as never before. Not only the campus but also traffic on all the surrounding roads leading to the court were jam-packed. The common wish sparkling in the eyes of everybody in the crowd was to get a glimpse of Fairy. Traffic police, city police, and CRPF were struggling very hard to maintain traffic mobility and Law & order situation. Police using PAS were continuously announcing requests for the public around to maintain peace.

Somehow, the police managed to drive Fairy's car to the main entrance gate of the Supreme Court. Despite all the precautions, the vigil failed to hide Fairy from the hunting eyes of the paparazzi's army and the audience crowd.

Teams of security guards and police safely escorted Fairy, her parents, Lawyer, and other associates from the main entrance gate to the designated court hall. Driving to the main gate and then escorting Fairy to the court hall was not an easy task, police been compelled intermittently to use force to clear the crowd.

And there, while being escorted moving too slowly to the designated court hall, complex emotions contouring the faces of Fairy & parents and the whole chronology being rolling down in their eyes like digital strings of films.....

On a haunted morning, a couple of days after that last reel, more precisely saying controversial provoking reel, the moment one police personnel knocked on the door and handed over the notice of the very first FIR to Fairy's father, the whole ambience of the house immensely shook up. Her mother started sobbing, and her father got brimmed. Fairy couldn't understand what exactly had happened. She took the FIR copy from her father's hands and tried to read it out repeatedly but couldn't understand much. So, she asked the parents about FIR; sobbing parents tried to explain but couldn't because of choked throats. Then she immediately started searching the internet to understand the nitty-gritty of FIR because the sad parents were finding it uncomfortable to explain the consequences.

The moment Fairy understood what it meant by FIR and what could-be the consequences, her adrenal pumped up. The internal body weather got disturbed to hormonals unbalancing, and soon she started feeling spewing sensations continuously intermittently.

At the same moment, her father started suffering from the attack of high blood pressure, heart-burning sensations, and breathing difficulty.

The brimmed mother finds herself helpless as to what to do? How do you handle the situation? How to take care of both daughter and husband who were gesturing as giving up emotionally and physically against the sudden disastrous fall out.

Somehow, while keeping herself cool, she immediately helped them with their routine medicines for medical emergency situations and sat with them, trying her level best to comfort them.

Not much time had passed since both Fairy and her father were brought to normal, and the doorbell rang again. All 3 looked into each other with a glimpse of suspicious fear; Mother asked them to sit quietly and stood up. She went out and opened the door; it was one more FIR from some other complainer.....one more jolt to the already dejected family. Both Fairy and Father again suffered attacks of their chronic ailments. Mother again started the routine process of first-aider treatments.

It was the hell day; it seemed so. Within a few hours of gaps, intermittently, FIRs were knocking at their doorstep, and few were received through emails as aftershocks Fairy, and her father were suffering the worst ever symptoms of ill health. Mother was trying her level best to manage everything, including herself and the deteriorating health conditions of Fairy and her father, but soon, she started feeling the situation unmanageable. So, she decided to call their family doctor.

Doctor Dhanvantarini was on leave that day for some important household work. She was not only a family doctor since the birth of Fairy, but in due course of time, she became a close family friend too, while treating Fairy. One interesting fact was that she was a renowned high-profile pediatrician in AIMS Indra Prasth. She was practicing as a family doctor only for Fairy, not any other patient. The reason was the abnormal, unique ailment of Fairy being diagnosed after her birth. Dr Dhanvantarini rushed very fast to Fairy's house, as she was staying in very close proximity to almost the neighboring society.

Dr Dhanvantarini acted quickly and succeeded in recovering both Fairy and Father to normal parameters. On the other hand, as a close family friend, somehow, she was well aware of Fairy's reels and her vibrant status as a social media celebrity. In due course of time she also became fan of Fairy.

Then, after going through all the FIRs and the current health traumatic state of the family, she consoled them and, as a confidence-building motivational gesture, assured them of the best legal help.

Then, without losing time, Dr Dhanvantarini called up renowned Supreme Court Lawyer Advocate Justitia, briefed her quickly about Fairy's background, her parents, her social media status, and the ongoing crisis in her life and requested legal help at the earliest. Advocate Justitia was on friendly and business terms with Dr Dhanvantarini as a Company Lawyer for many years. Advocate Justitia used to keep herself updated with things around, and in fact, was well aware of Fairy's reels and her social media popularity. Justitia was a high-profile Supreme Court Lawyer with a long list of VVIP and VIP Clients. But as a goodwill gesture, because of her close relationship with Dr Dhanvantarini and Fairy's medical condition of the specially-abled syndrome, Justitia spontaneously decided to take up that case without any hesitation. She cancelled her current post-lunch commitments and rushed to Fairy's place.

So, despite current adversities, the right things also fell into place at the right time for Fairy and their family.

Within a couple of hours, Advocate Justitia reached along with her few associates to Fairy's house.

The advocate and her team went through all the FIR documents and emails that Fairy had received and then checked Fairy's reels with microscopic perspectives. She and the team internally discussed a brief brainstorming strategic plan. Then, they finally shared their plan with Dr Dhanvantarini and Fairy's parents to immediately approach the Supreme Court for bail application. Because the IPC Sections under which charges had been imposed in all the FIRs were almost common and could lead to arrest at times. So, it is better first to apply for interim bail on high-priority. Then, after getting the bail, the application for aggregating all the cases coming from different parts of the country to a single court, that's the Supreme Court.

Fairy's parents and Dr Dhanvantarini nodded their heads in agreement.

As soon as the Lawyer and her team got ready to leave for the Supreme Court, the doorbell rang again.

It was a legal notice from one consortium of high-profile PIL activists from various religions sent through the Supreme Court. All got red and blue except Lawyer Justitia and the team.

So, that was the high time to take action on the dot.

Using her high-profile influence, Lawyer Justitia managed to get the Court's hearing for the interim bail against all the FIRs lodged so far and to club Fairy's appearing in the court the very next day against that high-profile PIL.

Because of being high-profile controversial case and shaky law-and-order situations in few parts of the country, the permanent bench of Supreme Court unanimously decided to take this case directly by Chief Justice of India.

Advocate Justitia managed to get high-priority for the case and reported it within the scheduled timeline. Her team managed to get front-row seats for Fairy & parents.

The entire hall was jam-packed with lawyers, petitioners, and an inquisitive crowd, including Fairy's fans.

As soon as Chief Justice Of India Shakti Kanungo appeared and approached the chair; everyone stood up with respect.

The Sr Court Assistant, Ms Vidyharti, placed all the documents and gadgets received so far from both sides on the table of the Chief Justice. Chief Justice took a longer while to go through the documents and then asked, "Defense Lawyer! Please come forward. Who is Fairy?"

Justitia stood from her seat and came forward, bowed down, owed respect, and responded quietly.

"Oh! Advocate Justitia, nice to see you again," Chief Justice chuckled with humor.

Then Justitia, who was standing in front of the Chief Justice, smiled back respectfully, turned back and signaled Fairy to stand up and come forward to appear.

Fairy looked at her parents, who were in praying posture and then followed the advocate, moved limpingly towards the bench of Chief Justice, "Namaste sir, I am Fairy.....," said in a wavering voice.

"So, you are Fairy. I saw you limping, and why is your voice shaky? Why? Are you ok?" asked Chief Justice.

"Yes sir, I am ok!" responded Fairy, again in shaky voice, seemed as lacking confidence.

"You are limping, your voice is trembling, but you are ok. But the situation in the country is not ok. Do you know why?" asked Chief Justice.

"……….," Fairy gone perplexed, and no words uttered.

He looked at Fairy for a few seconds, and then Chief Justice raised his voice, "Because of your provoking videos on social media. Do you know the dire consequences of the reaction? Do you know what could-be the punishment?"

Fairy's face turned red in response. Her hands and legs started shaking, her eyes started blinking rapidly, and her lips began to tremble.

The blunt words from Chief Justice were raising the turbulence in Fairy's mind and body, duly ignited by her chronicle ailment, adrenal started pumping erratically, hypothalamus seemed as going into state of disorder, and pituitary gland seemed as going imbalanced at releasing hormones…….the complex malfunction at the inside body environment, fueling up her especially abled syndrome, resulted into nausea and spewing sensations immediately.

Everybody around there in the court got surprised with sheer embarrassment at Fairy's such odd emetic symptoms, couple of times she appeared as feeling ashamed while controlling spewing attacks with eerie sound from her throat.

Suddenly, somebody from the front benches rushed to Fairy and started comforting her with a specific massage of her chest.

Chief Justice got annoyed at such a filthy & disgusting scenario in the court and yelled, "What's going on? Advocate Justitia, what's this?"

Advocate Justitia, with folded hands, responded as begging, "Sorry, My Lord! I beg your pardon. Actually Fairy is not a normal person like us, she is an especially abled person since her birth, that's why it all happened...."

But Chief Justice couldn't seem as convinced and slammed again, "What, sorry? And what is this especially abled person? If she is not well, then you shouldn't bring her to court. You are a highly experienced lawyer; you must have checked her health condition before appearing in court. You know very well that the police also don't arrest an accused if their health condition doesn't permit them. The Court can't continue like this." And gestured as picked up the hammer to declare adjournment of court.

Justitia interrupted in super-fast speed with folded hands as in a begging gesture and, before the Judge could have actioned, requested politely, "My Lord! Extremely sorry for the disturbance to the honorable court. But all this happened because of the urgency created by multiple FIRs. But, before concluding, please see the videos posted by Fairy and a brief about her health from her doctor."

"Hmmmm.....Ok.....Who is the doctor? Is the doctor present here in the court?" asked the Chief Justice while putting back the hammer on the table.

By that time, Fairy's condition was brought to normal by the doctor, and she was advised to sit comfortably with her parents. Justitia called up the doctor to appear and introduced her to the Chief Justice.

"So, you are doctor Dhanvantarini......very unique name. I never heard. Very classic and epic name....," chuckled the Chief Justice, this time with light humor. The doctor responded respectfully.

Chief Justice continued, "So, doctor, tell the court, what is the specially-abled factor of Fairy? What's wrong with her?"

The doctor responded with well-measured words, "My Lord! To understand, please allow me to 3 things. First, I need to present a summary of her chronological health reports for her chronic, specially-abled syndrome, which I brought for your reference. (Handed over that file to the court). Second, I need to be verbally brief about the same significantly. The third & final thing is that before proceeding with the first & second, watch Fairy's videos. That will help in understanding the whole issue holistically."

Before she could continue, Chief Justice interrupted, "OK! Then show the court those videos."

Advocate Justitia, with the help of court staff, logged in to her ALL $\forall$ account in the AI CI-enabled TV monitor and started showing the videos sequentially from Reel-1 to Reel-6.

The Chief Justice and the entire crowd in the court hall watched those videos, which created cult sensations for the last 14-15 years, making Fairy a most loved social media celebrity and now a culprit for disturbing the peace and harmony of this secular nation. Myriad expressions were interspersing at the curious face of Chief Justice while watching those videos. After watching those videos, he asked to show their properties. After a few while, the Chief Justice finally started a fresh spree of questions.

"Many questions....all need to be answered. So, doctor! Why does Fairy look so unstable in all the videos? See her body language, intoxicated facial expressions, drowsy eyes, shaky, choked voice, lack of confidence, and low energy.....means everything is messed up. Please enlighten the court on the exact deficiency or ailment. Is it autism or something like that?" Chief Justice asked the doctor.

But before the doctor could start, the Chief Justice interrupted, "Hold! Hold!! First answer against one interesting finding. I don't know how many have noticed or not. However, I noticed that there are 6 videos, and all were posted on a specific date only, and that was 03rd December, chronologically in a span of 14-15 years with intermittent gaps of a few years. The first reel was posted 15 years back on 03rd December; then the second reel was posted 14 years back on 03rd December, the third reel was posted 13 years back on 03rd December, then the fourth reel was posted 3 years back on 03rd December after a gap of 10 years, then fifth and sixth reels were posted on the same

day few days back from now in this year only on 03rd December…….
The question arises: Why is it only on 03rd December? What is the
unique significance of that particular date? What is the connection
between 03rd December and Fairy? And the last question in this set
of questions – where from Fairy got the idea or who actually helped to
create that peculiarly unique phrase 'Hi God, How Are You?'"

The question created peculiar curiosity among everybody in the crowd
except the doctor, Fairy, her parents, and her lawyers.

Doctor Dhanvantarini responded smilingly, "My Lord! 03rd December
is known as 'International Day Of Persons With Disabilities,' which
means, in better words,' International Day Of Especially Abled
Persons.'"

"Oh!" sighed Chief Justice, "Interesting!!!"

The doctor continued, "In addition to that, 03rd December is the
birth date of Fairy. So, now one can understand that it's an emotional
connection of 03rd December with Fairy. That's why initially her parents
and then later on she chose to post reels on 03rd December only."

"Oh! Interesting. Let's discuss this in detail later. Now please tell me
the reasons for her especially abled issue," Chief Justice expressed.

"My Lord! Sir, actually Fairy was born with one rarest of rare diseases
that is called 'Auto Brewery Syndrome'…..," doctor said…..

Before the doctor could have continued the judge again interrupted,
"Auto Brewery Syndrome! What's that? Never heard before….Please
explain in lay man's language, easy words. Not in professional medical
language using complex words. So that court can understand and also
people present in the court."

There was a mass sigh in the hall in reaction.

"Sure, sir. Actually, a detailed medical report is handed over to the
court for anytime reference. Now, let me explain it in user-friendly
language. 'Auto Brewery Syndrome' is a condition in which alcohol is
produced in the stomach. Whenever and whatever the patient eats

or drinks, everything is converted into alcohol. Even if the stomach is empty, the digestive juices and hormones get converted into alcohol."

It's a rare health condition, and there are rare patients in the world suffering from this syndrome. Mostly, it's underdiagnosed in many cases. And mostly incurable, too, except for a few countable exceptions. Few handful cases are in the history of modern medical science where doctors succeed in maintaining low severity of the syndrome, i.e., low blood alcohol levels in a few fortunate patients. And survival rate is also low in such patients.

There are limited facts and figures available in the medical history about this syndrome. Everything is included in the report submitted.

Those unfortunate patients who couldn't be cured were helpless to lead a life suffering from multiple chronic complex symptoms like vomiting, belching, dizziness, drowsiness, alcohol hangover, disorientation, irritable bowel syndrome, loss of coordination, neurological disorders, anxiety, depression, chronic fatigue syndrome, lack of concentration, lack of focus, psychological disorders, frequent mood swings, bipolar disorder, etc....

So is the case of my patient, Fairy. She has been unstable since her birth. 'Auto Brewery Syndrome' was diagnosed in the early stage after her birth. She had undergone various treatments of modern medical science & technology, but unfortunately, nothing worked significantly. Meanwhile, ageing made the ailment more complex and caused more suffering. She was in need of much-balanced treatment, as her survival was always a huge challenge for us.

For all these years, my team of doctors and I have been continuously putting all possible efforts into bringing down the severity of blood alcohol levels and behavioral disorders. Her parents were putting all their effort into her better upbringing.

You can see that despite all those obstacles, she learned and successfully made her first reel when she was merely 3 years old. Can you believe a child born with severe disease and disabilities could make a rhyme as a reel in her own words?"

"Hold! Hold!!" interrupted the Chief Justice, "How can you say that the rhymes in the reels are made by Fairy, even at a very early age of 3, 4, and 5? To me, it seems that the rhymes are written by her parents, not made by Fairy."

At the tender age of 3, it is quite impossible for a child-like Fairy to have an understanding of such issues of God, prayer, abnormal, new normal, doctor, deaf, dumb, blind, and rhyming of words. Similarly, at the age of 4, the words like especially abled, stepchildren, lifetime disorder, karma, feath and the matured contents of reel 2. Then, quite mature content of reel 3 was posted at the age of 5. From the 4th reel onwards, one can consider the maturity level to create such rhymes. But, still, when she dropped out of school, as mentioned in the 3rd reel, how could she learn all these things without going to school or college? Court wants to know the truth?"

"My Lord! I can't answer all. Better to ask her parents....please," humbly responded the doctor.

"Ok! Please call Fairy's parents," Chief Justice ordered.

Fairy's parents came forward to the bench of Chief Justice.

"So, you are parents? Please introduce yourself to the court," asked the judge.

"Sir, I am Raj Kumar, Fairy's father,"

"Sir, I am Jasoda Devi, Fairy's mother,"

"Ok! So, Raj and Jasoda, whatever is told by the defense lawyer and the family doctor, I am unable to understand what kind of upbringing and education you have provided to your especially abled child? She dropped out of school as per the reel 3. But, even before that, how could she make 2 reels at a very tender age? Is that popular phrase 'Hi God, How Are You?' created by you, and she just sang? Without any formal school education, how could she be able to mention serious social issues in her rhymes? It seemed highly suspicious that all rhymes are written by you, and she just sang?" asked the Chief Justice.

Furious eyes of Raj and Jasoda stared into each other as they talked something mutually, and then Jasoda came forward and responded, "My Lord! Let me explain everything that will clear all the suspicions. Sir, born as an abnormal child with a rare disease, not only the poor physical health of Fairy was painful, but more than that, her unstable mental health was more challenging. A little bit of stress or uneasiness did cause spewing sensations. Her childish mood swings and behavioral traits were more disturbing. We could never predict what way she will act or respond...."

"Fairy was very much unpredictable; things were happening as per the severity levels of blood alcohol...," the doctor intervened.

The judge just gave a grave look at the doctor and then turned his eyes towards Jasoda, who continued, "Yes, sir, she was highly unpredictable, and it still often happens with her. So, just as an optional practical solution to keep her busy to get rid of her psychological turmoil, we put one of our cell phones in her tiny hands at such a tender age of 1.5/2 years......though TV was there, we found that she was more comfortable with a cell phone. To our surprise, even being a toddler, she was taking immense interest in operating cells and watching a variety of stuff. She used to get upset whenever we tended to take her cell from her hands or when she was not getting any stuff to please her. And that worked out to reduce her anxiety levels."

So, somehow reluctantly, we continued to carry on her newfound way of keeping herself emotionally stable, busy, and happy in her own way. But then more than that, we treated it as an opportunity to train her for many things, like identifying various things, playing with logic, mindful games of children, identifying and speaking letters, words, names, sets of words, small sentences, numbers, colors, and many things as generally parents do for normal children.

Even though the doctor advised us to balance usage as screen time limits, that wasn't the alarming issue with Fairy. Because of just a few minutes of screen time, she used to get drowsiness and napping sensations because of fluctuating blood alcohol levels and then used to sleep for a while intermittently. Also, at the same time, to avoid any chronic neurological or psychological disorders, we didn't force Fairy and allowed to do whatever she wanted. Because if, at any point of time, we tried to intervene in her cell activities immediately, she used to start spewing. The best part was she used to ask questions whenever she did find something new or interestingly intriguing. That way, she started learning whatever she came across on the cell.

Surprisingly, before attaining the 3rd year, she learned so many things about her birthday, a special day of the specially-abled, love, doctor, God, prayer, normal, abnormal, brother, sister, counting a little bit, videos, reels, chat, posting, etc. etc. And while her 3rd birthday stubbornly she started asserting for making her own reel. We were curious and asked her what you would say in the video, but she was not saying anything but to start making her video. When asked where you will post? Children are not allowed in any app. But then she insisted on finding an app where she could directly record and post her reel. After a little search, we find this app ALL $\forall$. And then when we started shooting, we were surprised like hell…..the very first words from her mouth stunned us……Hi God, How Are You?…..then she glibly went on singing like an aspiring singer, you know….daddy was shooting and holding the cell, and I was just guiding her, signaling for a move here and there and for changing her postures……..despite her acute disabilities, she completed her first video of length approx. 2 minutes……

Her words, fluidity, rhyming, style of raising her issues, the unique way of calling God……everything that happened just shocked us beyond surprise. And then, when it was posted, the unpredictable huge response stunned us. She became like a celebrity overnight. Despite being a toddler, she could feel her newly earned popularity, and we felt that helped in combating neurological, psychological, and emotional turbulences in her system. However, all the physical problems continued as before.

Then afterwards, during the whole year, she never reiterated making a reel; she just kept on enjoying watching her reel and responses pouring in. We don't know how much she understood, but whenever she asked us anything against any comment, we just explained in simple words without any prejudices.

Then, after one year, on 03rd December, on her 4th birthday, she again started asserting to make a reel. In her 2nd reel, she also started talking to God and asked many questions. Whatever she sang, everything was her own creation using the knowledge she earned while her cell stints, not a single bit of input from us. Surprisingly, she sang in one stretch. That reel also went viral on huge scale.

Then, the next year, she was admitted to 1st standard in a nearby school. Actually, we didn't put her in kindergarten school because of her health conditions, so we directly admitted her to primary school. Unfortunately, she couldn't do well in school. Because of her strange body language and quirky behavior, she was often targeted to make fun of and teased by fellow students and seniors, and those embarrassments resulted in mental trauma, leading to vomiting in the classroom and on the school campus. Those vomiting incidents resulted in a lot of complaints from the school and warnings also to get her health in order. Sometimes, we felt that she liked going to school despite the nuisances she was facing there, but that school was not comfortable with her physical and behavioral traits. Finally, she dropped out after a couple of months.

We tried a lot to get admitted to other schools in the city, but we couldn't get admission. Then, the doctor helped with admission to a school for specially-abled children. In that school also, Fairy couldn't continue and dropped out again. So, we were left without any option other than teaching her through online classes. But that also couldn't work out properly because of her health issues. Somehow, we continued the membership in those online classes, and it all depended on her health and mood when she spent time studying. Meanwhile, she used to spend time with her cell phone and started taking an interest in watching TV programmes.

Meanwhile, that year, after 2 school dropouts, on 03rd December, she again reiterated making reels. This time, we weren't surprised because of knowing the fact that she loves to talk to God on this precious day of 3rd December every year when, coincidently, her birthday coincides with the special day for specially-abled people. This time, in her 3rd reel, she was asking God questions about her dropouts, similar cases where many children are deprived of education because of a variety of reasons, such as birthright of health & education. Surprisingly, that reel was also a super hit on social media.

As far as the seriousness or maturity of her contents is concerned, all were her spontaneously rhymed stuff, not a little bit of preparation or any input from parents……and that surprised not only the world but also parents. Whatever she was learning from us, her cell stints, TV Programmes, and then online classes, she might be using in her own way.

"Sir, sorry to interrupt again. Actually, medical science acknowledged that disability also brings some specialties. Fairy is a live example. Her brain somehow developed the art of using subconscious memories into spontaneous rhyming," The doctor intervened. Chief Justice just gave a grave look, and then Jasoda continued.

Yes sir, the doctor is right.

Then, in the next many years, she never forced us to make reels on that precious day of 03rd December. She didn't even answer our questions about not making reels. We thought it might be her mood swings or something she didn't want to share with us. But there were also many surprises; she used to make reels whenever she liked to make them but never posted them on ALL.

Throughout those years, most of our time was wasted on her chronic disease, in between; somehow, whenever health permitted, she used to spend time on online studies also, like homeschooling but rarely appeared in exams because exams were highly stressful for her, creating unbearable turbulence in her mind and body. We also used to teach her about our daily habits, routine chores, mother tongue, Hindi, English language, ancestral cultural heritage, Sanskrit, the history of our nation, Bharat, our Sanatan Dharma, our Gods and worships, world history, other religions in the world, little bit maths, and many things from contemporary textbooks.

But I don't know what's going on inside her brain; since the very first time when she started making reels, she sang in English, not in her mother tongue, Hindi, and used to say, 'Hi God' instead of 'He Bhagwan.' Whenever we asked about the reasons behind it, she would get irritated. Only once did she respond surprisingly, saying that the Gods of all religions are ultimately one single unique God, and humanity is the only religion above all so-called religions, which are actually ways of life in different ways. I love that unique God only and love to talk and play with it.

Then, after many years, on her 15th birthday, she wished to make a reel. Though she made many reels after that popular 3rd reel but didn't post. But this time, when she covered a lot of social and global issues while singing her spontaneous rhymes, we were badly surprised while shooting. Even though she was highly inconsistent, but that 4th reel, after a long gap of more than 10 years, created history again and broke all the past records of social media for all the parameters such as viewership, likes, comments and sharing. Like her fans, we were also dumbfounded by her concerns and what exactly goes on in her mind. At her age, people generally have childish interests, but whenever she opened herself up to the world, mature, serious issues came out of her mouth, which was really stunning.

As parents, we were very happy to see her happy face after every successful reel. Though we never ever could understand the reasons behind the success of her reels, as golden words say, 'nothing succeeds like success,' we often just wished for her life to be fulfilled with endless success; maybe that could heal our child from that deadly disease of 'Auto Brewery Syndrome.'

Then again, there was a gap of 3 years when she didn't post any reel.

After 3 years, it was again a rare coincidence; this time, her birthday & special day coincided with the election period, and she was voting for the first time. In fact, voting was over in the last week of November, but after watching her next reels, the 5th & 6th, it seemed that she was eagerly waiting for the date, 03rd December, to make and post her next reel.

The 5th reel we shot in the morning and Fairy indicatively covered issues of election, democracy, secularism, religion-based political campaigns, and Hindu - Muslim conflicts. She even asked whether God do voting. One can guess her unpredictable IQ levels, even at the age of 18, by the questions she used to ask. Soon after posting, that reel went viral.

But that day, after some time, she again asserted for making one more reel by saying that she missed a few very important issues related to elections and wanted to cover today itself. So, the sixth reel was made in the evening and was posted immediately. To our surprise, the sixth reel also flooded with views and went viral hugely. In that reel, she covered electoral violence and Hindu-Muslim controversies plaguing social life and the nation and asked God to resolve the perennial conflict.

Aside from the election centered unrest, things were going normal. But the environment started heating up within a few hours overnight, when we started getting threatening DMs and messages on ALL and then after a few more hours, news of hatred against Fairy started airing on News channels, and debate programmes started over Fairy's reels and after effects. Then after few hours we started getting legal notices, FIR's......and then finally we are here Sir, in honorable court.......that's all from our side.

Jasoda Devi's statement was too long, made the Chief Justice feeling so bored and irritated. But somehow he managed to hear, as Jasoda was speaking very fluently.

"Hmmm.....isn't your statement so long? Unnecessarily!.......it might be recorded as one of the longest statements ever in history. You might have said preciously in short form. Just for the sake of justice, the court heard it patiently," Chief Justice reacted with annoyance.

Then he continued with curiosity, "BTW, one thing I noticed. The whole statement was given by you only, Fairy's father Raj Kumarji stood silent throughout the time. What was the reason?"

"My Lord! Raj has chronic high BP issues, that's why. Actually, after Fairy's birth, because of her painful health issues, he suffered strokes of migraine and hyper stress, which ultimately caused high BP. So, generally, he used to keep silent, and I handle any conversations," responded Jasoda in a softer voice.

"Oh! Ok!!.....So now you can take your seats," sympathetically reverted the Chief Justice.

Both Raj and Jasoda bowed down in respect and moved back to accompany Fairy in the front-row.

Then, the Chief Justice just turned his head around and uttered, "The Court has seen all the evidences, the documents, videos and heard the statements. But still, the court is not convinced to grant the bail. Something is missing somewhere. Still, the court has all the doubts that reels are not the brainchild of Fairy, but of her parents......."

Advocate Justitia gestured as intervening by raising hands in defense and uttered as the Chief Justice immediately allowed, "My Lord! Fairy's chronic health condition is the sole reason behind seeking bail. The question of who created the rhymes is secondary and could-be debated while hearing in the next sessions. So, it's my humble request to grant bail to my client…..”

“Objection, My Lord…..,” a heavy voice echoed from the other side. Everybody looked at the lawyer who raised an objection.

With raised eyebrows, the Chief Justice intervened, “You are…..”

“My Lord! I am advocate Daya Swami, lawyer of petitioner of PIL, seeking for harshest punishment to the accused Fairy……,” the lawyer from opposition reverted loudly.

“Ok! Wait a minute….,” the Chief Justice just reacted. And then started going through the PIL documents and other multiple FIRs.

After a while, the Chief Justice addressed, “So your PIL and other's FIRs, all are seeking prosecution under IPC Sections 295A, 153, 153A and 67…….and charges under all these sections are not bailable. Ok, the court wants to know your reasons behind labelling these sections.”

Lawyer Daya Swami responded, “My Lord! The charges are self-explanatory. The contents in the videos, particularly the 6th video, had all the potential for intentionally & maliciously hurting religious sentiments, for creating provocation to riots, for promoting disharmony or enmity between 2 religious communities, and for posting satirical content. Altogether for disturbing peace and harmony of our society,”

“Don't go hypothetical. Word by word, you have to prove whatever you mentioned in your petition and whatever you are verbally telling the court…….,” the Chief Justice slammed.

“Yes, My Lord! My client Maulana Khan will explain…..,” Lawyer Daya responded. The Chief Justice signaled to go ahead.

Maulana Khan bowed down in respect and uttered, “My Lord! A few things mentioned are against Islam…….firstly, *‘Muslims say only their God is great,’* second line,” *please come down and decide whose God is great.’* Sir, our holy book says that ‘Allah is the Greatest’ and nobody is allowed to deny it. Then, such statements are like blasphemy, which intentionally hurts Muslim sentiments.

Then the statement, *'God created human' said old wise, 'human created God' said new wise. I am again confused, please clarify who created whom when and why?* My Lord! Our holy book says that it's Allah who has created the world and any such statement challenging our scripture is intolerable to us.

Moreover, in all her videos, the way she calls God, *'Hi God! How are you?'* is derogatory and an insult to our Allah. God must be called with respectful words and in obedience.

As the representative from the Muslim community, I strongly condemn the intentionally stated malicious contents against Islam and request the court to prosecute the culprit and give the harshest punishment..."

Chief Justice just smiled and reciprocated, "Mr Maulana! You talked about just a few lines suiting you, but there are many other lines that loudly speak about other pitfalls. The court respects all religions and all human beings. The court can't see a case from a single lens. The court will evaluate the potential of every aspect through an unprejudiced prosecution process with due diligent participation and debates from everybody involved. It's a democratic country; everybody has the right to freedom of expression, but without hurting the essence of democracy. Don't worry; the court assures you of protecting your religious interests and neutral justice to all."

"Right now, the Court is prima fascia focusing on the bail application issue."

Advocate Daya and Maulana both intervened almost at the same time, "Sir! We oppose bail to the accused. She might repeat offending public sentiments by posting malicious contents again....,"

"Don't waste court's time with your old-fashioned legal tactics. It is the court's prerogative to control the actions of an accused. The Court has listened to your arguments, both legal and religious contents. The court assures you of proper prosecution in the coming days. Right now, the court should focus on the bail. Law and court are not there only to punish people, but to save innocent from undue punishment," the annoyed Chief Justice groaned.

Then immediately turned to the defense lawyer, "To get the bail, the single reason for poor health is not adequate enough. When the accused can make videos while suffering from such poor health conditions, then why can't she adjust herself in the police remand or jail? Or otherwise, her parents? As earlier said, the court wants to know the truth. Who is the creator of rhymes? Fairy or parents? Please prove if you want bail……"

Advocate Justitia just got tensed, and immediate brainstorming started in her mind.

There were whispers in the court……meanwhile, Jasoda, who was watching curiously, stood up from her place and moved towards Justitia. She whispered something in her ears and came back. Jasoda's words brought a smile to her face, and as soon as she was about to speak, the annoying Chief Justice, amid the nuisance of whispering pollution, thumped the hammer, "Order! Order!!……silence. Yes, Ms Defense Lawyer, please go ahead….."

Justitia, with loads of confidence, "My Lord! If the court permits, can we call Fairy for a live demo to prove the truth….."

"Oh! What an idea!! I thought that you would propose a lie-detector test for Fairy and their parents. But that would have taken a lot of time, rather a lot of days. BTW, this is a better idea. Please call Fairy, but before that, please ensure any medication if required to avoid any embarrassing spewing……," chuckled the Chief Justice.

Advocate Justitia moved towards the front bench, where Fairy was sitting along with her parents and the family doctor. As the doctor heard the words of the Chief Justice, she gave pills to Fairy as a preventive measure for spewing and stress-busting. Then Fairy, along with Justitia, moved towards the bench of Chief Justice.

This time Chief Justice gestured with befriending smile on his face and welcomed, "Fairy! How are you?"

Fairy was pleasantly surprised at such a soft gesture and smiled back, "I am fine Sir....."

"Good....well, Fairy! You are very popular for the lovely songs in your videos. Now I want to see a live song from you. Can you sing a song for Judge Uncle......," Chief Justice expressed tactfully but straightly came to the point.

Fairy nodded her head in yes and asked, "What topic?"

"Ha ha ha.....any topic....may be current scenario around you," the Chief Justice softly uttered.

"Ok Sir!....," she responded smilingly and closed her eyes for a while.

A few seconds later, her eyes opened with a confident jerk, and then......

Hi God! How are you?
I am in the court, need your support.
See, my Mom and Dad are crying,
No help from you, but still praying.
Accusers say I am anti God and abused you,
Tell them it's not true, you know I love you.
Am I wrong? Asking you questions?
It's my style to get your connection!
Please come here and remove all religiophobia,
Spread LOVE everywhere, make Humanity only tobia!!!
Today if you won't come, I will be Katti!
Today if you won't help, I will never be batti!!
What a mellifluous rhyme!!!

So, it was Fairy.

The cult of social media.

The goddess of miracle words.

The goddess of rhymes, who spontaneously and fearlessly sings whatever comes into her mind.

The specially-abled blessing to the parents and to this world, who speak the truth without fearing powerful pseudos' from any walk of life, maybe politics, religion, or society.

It was a pin-drop silence while Fairy was singing…..

But then, as soon as she gestured as finished, loud whispers started echoing 'hhsssshhh,' 'wwooooossshhhh,' 'wowww'…….and soon within a few seconds, the entire court hall was thundered with loud claps.

Everybody stood in a standing ovation, surprisingly, including the honorable Chief Justice. Historically, it has happened for the first time when a judge, moreover the Chief Justice, was paying a standing ovation in the court, also to an accused.

The huge loads of applause continued way beyond limits.

After few minutes people heard, "Order! Order!!…..," amid the echoing sounds of powerful clapping.

Thunderous applause began to subside gradually, but the Chief Justice wasn't comfortable and again yelled, "Order! Order!!…..,"

Somehow, the high-energy noise of applause came to a normal level.

BTW few exceptions were also there who got badly irritated not by noise but by huge applauds and didn't participate intentionally for the best reasons known to them.

"Ha ha ha……So, what an amazing experience! For the first time in my life, I witnessed such a live performance full of spontaneous talent, also from an accused, to prove innocence. Impressed with an innovative way of calling unified God…….Though it was a short rhyme, it was very meaningful with a huge message……BTW, Fairy! What's that katti batti and why?" Chief Justice broke the silence on a lighter note.

Fairy smiled and whispered in her peculiar, hushed voice, "Sir! While playing, children often do katti, which means breaking a friendship if they are not happy with each other. And then do batti, means befriending when wish to befriend again……..So, the same I was telling God if my request will not be listened"

Fairy's answer was liked by many but also hated by few.

"Ha ha ha……ok…..," Chief Justice smiled.

Then, after a brief pause, the Chief Justice authoritatively announced, "So, finally considering all the evidences and witnesses, the court grants unconditional bail, rather than blanket bail to the accused Fairy, against all the submitted PILs, FIRs and other complaints, and even against any future petitions in connection with the videos posted by Fairy on the app ALL. However, prosecution will continue, and the schedule will be intimated in due course of time. Moreover, considering the health grounds, Fairy will be provided respite from appearing in court; her presence in the court will not be mandatory at any point of time. However, the designated lawyers will have to ensure their presence in the court during prosecution proceedings." He thumped the bench with a hammer, stood up and headed to his cabin.

Everybody bowed down in respect and started dispersing.

Majority in the audience respected the judgement and started shouting slogans, 'Bharat Mata Ki Jay,' 'Vande Matram,' 'Jay Shree Ram,' 'Hindustan Jindabad,' 'Fairy Jindabad'……….but as usual few were feeling offended unnecessarily.

Amid dense crowd Fairy, her parents, doctor, and lawyer under police protection been escorted out of the court into their vehicle. But roads were jam-packed. Everybody in the crowd with their might were trying to get a glimpse of Fairy.

A lot of time was wasted, and traffic was almost at a standstill. Fairy's car was being badly surrounded by fans who were trying to get a glimpse.

Finally the escorting police officer in the car suggested to open the roof deck panel and Fairy to stand to make her appearing to the restless crowd. They followed his advice and then Fairy along with her parents stood up. Fairy stood in between the parents and started waving hands with smile, cheering the fans. Fans were also waving hands and shouting slogans.......

The good thing was that traffic started moving.....

Thaaaad.......thaaaad.......thaaaad.......thaaaad.....

Suddenly, huge sounds shocked everybody around......

Then the parents and people around noticed that suddenly Fairy's head rolled off to the other side and she started sinking down, suddenly blood streams spilt out from her head and mouth, her cries stuck in her throat.......parents screamed out.....so the fans nearby the car......somehow parents started trying to manage to bring her down below inside the car.

The police crew escorting the car came into action and started dispersing the crowd away.

The doctor accompanying them came into action and started First Aid and arrangements for an Ambulance.

Meanwhile the police quickly found that 4 stones struck there, one on Fairy's head and 3 on car. But clueless from where the stones rammed into.

The fan crowd was losing its patience and started shouting painful cries.....

Suddenly, the day's good vibes turned into a horrific nightmare.....

As usual, the police were busy in damage control as post-incident action, though it happened right away in their presence only........

The whole incident, as breaking news, went viral within a few minutes on TV news channels and all social media channels, it captured more heat than today's court proceeding and judgement for bail......

Soon debates started airing on TV news channels encashing the golden opportunity. Social media channels including ALL too followed the trend.......

Lots of wild thoughts are making rounds in the public mind.....

Will Fairy survive or not? Time will tell.....

But when can such stone pelting be stopped?

The appeasement politics out of pseudo secularism empower stone pelting by democracy abusers.....

One who neutrally outspeaks the truth is often silenced....

Democracy is a privilege not only for the abusers but for candid users also.....

Justice from the Law and Court goes in vain by unjustice from the shady laws of parallel Courts......

Last but not the least....

What could Fairy have said if not fallen unconscious after being hit by insanely pelted stones.....

Hi God, how are you?

Hi God, why are you?

As usual, God might remain invisible and silent.......

............How long will stone pelting continue???

............Wake-up, Indians.....Wake up!!!

............Wake-up, World......Wake up!!!